Beyond Blair Witch

Also by N.E. Genge

The Unofficial X-Files Companion

The Unofficial X-Files Companion II

The Unofficial X-Files Companion III

The X-Files Lexicon

Millennium: The Unofficial Companion (vol. 1)

Millennium: The Unofficial Companion (vol. 2)

The Buffy Chronicles: The Unofficial Companion to Buffy the Vampire Slayer

Urban Legends: The As-Complete-As-One-Could-Be Guide to Modern Myths

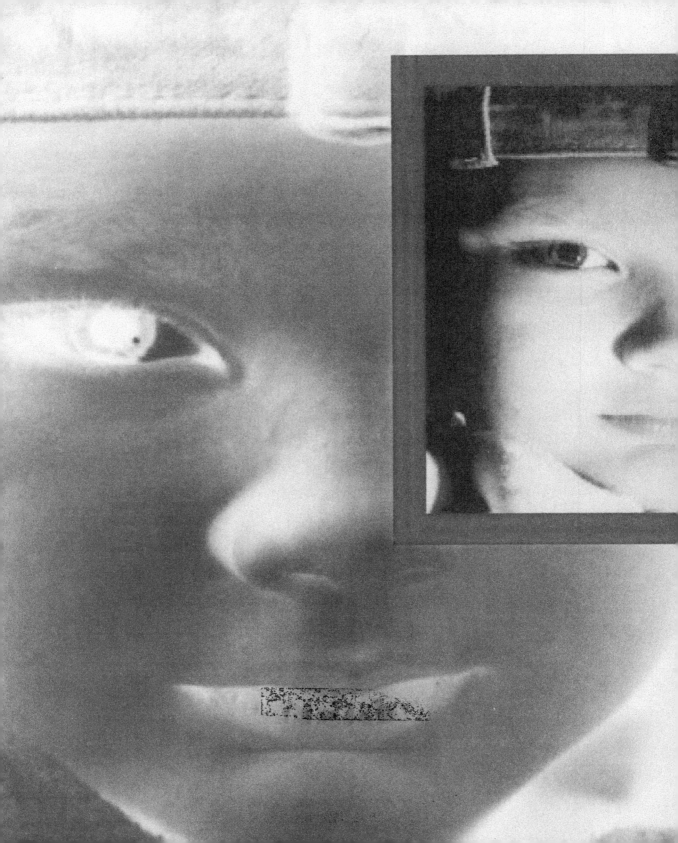

Beyond Blair Witch

The Haunting of America

from the Carlisle Witch

to the Real Ghosts

of Burkittsville

N. E. GENGE

THREE RIVERS PRESS · NEW YORK

Text copyright © 2000 by N.E. Genge
Photographs copyright © 2000 by N.E. Genge

Published by Three Rivers Press, New York, New York. Member of the Crown Publishing Group.

Random House, Inc. New York, Toronto, London, Sydney, Auckland
www.randomhouse.com

THREE RIVERS PRESS is a registered trademark and the Three Rivers Press colophon is a trademark of Random House, Inc.

Printed in the United States of America

Design by Kay Schuckhart/Blond on Pond

Library of Congress Cataloging-in-Publication Data

Genge, Ngaire.
    Beyond Blair Witch : the haunting of America from the Carlisle Witch to the real ghosts of Burkittsville / by N.E. Genge.—1st ed.
        p. cm.
    ISBN 0-609-80645-9 (pbk.)
    1. Ghosts—United States. I. Title.

BF1472.U6 G45 2000
133.1'0973—dc21   00-036464

ISBN 0-609-80645-9

10 9 8 7 6 5 4 3 2 1

First Edition

For Peter and for Michael, who still listen

contents

acknowledgments

Though writing is an inherently lonely occupation, no book comes into being without the help of many other people. There's the obvious assistance from the professionals who undertake the monumental task of taking the original box full of paper and illustrations and turning it into an elegantly edited, designed, and printed book. There's the day-to-day support of family and friends who endure the long silences to help celebrate the completion of each section. But there's also the much more subtle influence of centuries of other writers whose stories provide inspiration as well as the wonderful—and sobering—realization that while each new effort is done alone, it is also part of a timeless endeavor that continues, virtually unchanged despite technology or fashion, to explore and entertain. In this book, I find myself uniquely indebted to all three groups, so it's with great delight that I can publicly thank:

Patty Gift and all the wonderful people who work with her for their enthusiasm, long hours, flexibility, and attention to detail.

Ling Lucas for finding this book such a wonderful home.

Mike O'Neill for making sure that the box of paper and illustrations looked so wonderful.

Lorna Sainsbury for managing the chaos and tracking down everything from historical dates to a really good cup of coffee without complaint.

Peter LeBlanc, Eliza Pittman, Gail Vokey, and all the other oral storytellers mentioned by name in the following pages. The Yarnspinners of Eastern Canada who help keep spoken word storytelling alive and well, for hanging on to the stories that might otherwise be lost. The overworked and unappreciated people who mount UnCONventional, Come Here 'Til I Tell You, and numerous other storytelling festivals each year, for letting me listen in and pointing me to some of the most delightful people it's been my experience to work with.

And, of course, to Peter and Michael, who love the tales as much as I do—and who willingly wash dishes, tackle laundry, and do whatever else it takes to help me get them down on paper. Thank you.

Beyond Blair Witch

introduction

"It's just so *real!*"

When *The Blair Witch Project*'s principal actors appeared following the film's debut at Sundance, audiences gasped—then cheered. Not because the three young actors had managed to clean up so well after an eight-day shoot—without showers or regular meals—in the backwoods of Maryland, but because they were alive at all!

The Blair Witch Project, the "mockumentary" that was shot for a mere $25,000 (or $33,000, or $60,000, depending on which publication and expense sheet you read) and then went on to make nearly $1.6 million in its first weekend, makes much of its fictional "reality."

Real actors contributed their names to the three fictional filmmakers.

Those herky-jerky onscreen images, which remind at least one viewer per showing of a childhood tendency toward motion sickness, were shot by three amateurs.

And Burkittsville, Maryland, much to the current consternation of its residents, is a real community.

It's in Burkittsville that the fact and fantasy that mingled so successfully in *The Blair Witch Project* are most clearly separated once again. Just days after the film's release, the town council of Burkittsville voted to increase police presence in the tiny community, especially at the old graveyard where parts of *The Blair Witch Project* were shot (without the usual irksome location issues—items such as permission from the town or the community's churches). A sudden influx of fans, all looking for the "historical" sites depicted in the film, overwhelmed residents and police officers, who found themselves confronted by frustrated people flatly refusing to believe that Blair Witch was nothing more than the imagining of Eduardo Sánchez and Daniel Myrick. One young woman publicly accused the town of "covering up the true events" to "avoid bad publicity"; her traveling companion, a self-declared neo-pagan, suggested that it was time for the community to "come clean," as Salem had, and, instead of "denying their history," that the residents of Burkittsville should "embrace their Wiccan past and erect a proper memorial to Elly Kedward."

An exit survey outside the Bridge Theater revealed that seven of every ten viewers believed the legend of the Blair Witch. Five of every ten believed that the Blair Witch—or at least Elly Kedward—was a documented historical figure. Were directors Sánchez and Myrick such cinematic geniuses that they could hoodwink thousands?

No. Not at all. As the two freely admit, they were as startled as anyone else when absolute strangers began publicly attesting to the film's validity. Claims that the Blair Witch was a real person left Sánchez and Myrick shaking their heads, delighted that their prerelease activities had generated the much-needed buzz to propel the film into general release but baffled by the vehemence brought to both sides of the argument. As they told anyone willing to listen, they were simply playing to a public already primed by nearly three hundred years of campfire tales that left listeners quivering in their sleeping bags to accept this story.

Elly Kedward, their amalgamation of the central figures of so many of America's wicked witch legends, drew on a uniquely New World set of tales that, though repeated orally all over the eastern United States for three centuries, had yet to be showcased for the mass media. What Bram Stoker, Anne Rice, Poppy Z. Brite, and others had previously done for vampires, Sánchez and Myrick had now done for colonial witches.

Their tale galvanized all the previously free-floating images, themes, and motifs one might expect of this genre into a single story, a story they then proceeded to present in a totally new format—film—using techniques that, though unnerving, proved a perfect partnership for their images. That Haxan Films could expand the "reality" of the environment they'd created into the "supporting documents" and "evidence" on *The Blair Witch Project*'s companion Web site, that the Web site was evidently always meant to be considered an integral part of the viewing experience (in fact, much of the film remains slightly incomprehensible *without* the Web site), only serves to illustrate the genre's stability as a distinct, recognizable literary entity. Regardless of the medium, the essential story is so much a part of our group awareness that, even in totally unexpected surroundings, it continues to draw us in, to whisper those never-quite-forgotten campfire legends in our ear.

We believe.

We believe because the most powerful frames of this film, though a totally modern creation, draw on our oldest fears—the things that went bump in the nights of our childhoods. We've been hearing bits of the Blair Witch legend all our lives! The incredible resonance the film created with its audience stems from a uniquely American version of what Jung called the "collective unconscious," a set of symbols, fears, even dreams, peopled by archetypes—what Hollywood calls stereotypes. By deliberately tweaking those memories and bringing them to the fore,

Sánchez and Myrick could leave us sitting in pitch-black theaters and *know* that every person in those seats was filling the darkened screen with the same terrors.

It's the haunting familiarity, the commonality of those terrors, the shared experience of America's occult legends, that allowed viewers to whisper, "I *know* I've seen *that* before!" to one another as the stickmen twirled in the breeze. This despite the fact that this evocative figure is more modern than the Nike swoosh!

Considering the instinctive recognition of the wicked witch imagery and themes evidenced by *Blair Witch Project* audiences, you might expect to find massive tomes of reference material floating about in local libraries. You won't. Like the urban legends that circulated in spoken form for decades before anyone thought to gather them into comprehensive written collections, most of America's witch tales remain oral accounts.

The stories that follow, many presented for the first time in written form, track down the memory fragments and splinters of story that *The Blair Witch Project* used to such powerful effect. It is time to reintroduce those eldritch tales that continue to tickle our imaginations and identify the historical and folkloric archetypes that have been recast in the Blair Witch mythos, causing thousands to believe that Elly Kedward might still reach out to drag unsuspecting students into the Maryland woods.

Here are the tales that inspired the most common comment outside the theaters showing *The Blair Witch Project:* "But I *know* I've heard of something like that happening *somewhere!* Remember when . . ."

the winter shun

The outsider, the alien among us, the character who, for whatever reason, is segregated from society, fulfills two distinct purposes in fiction by providing not only the yardstick by which the larger group is judged—and which group inevitably judges itself superior in comparison—but by reflecting, without distortion, each individual's personal fear of rejection.

Even in the midst of exercising its ultimate power—the ability to dehumanize its own—the majority is threatened by the outcasts they create. A certain "there but for the grace of God go I" feeling envelops the shunned, inevitably arousing the fear that a like fate could await any one of those who would sanction such punishment in the first place. This dichotomy, the tension born between the desire to exert power and the misgivings aroused by establishing such precedents, allows the outcast to inspire both contempt and fear, and even a bizarre form of awe.

Nowhere is the pariah's ability to evoke simultaneous hatred and respect more evident than in the witch tales of colonial America. *The Blair Witch Project*'s title character, Elly Kedward, driven from her home on the say-so of mere children, traditionally the least powerful citizens, is clearly impotent within her community. Whatever powers she was accused of trafficking, while sufficient to get her thrown out in midwinter, aren't threatening enough to leave fictional Blair's residents quivering in their boots or avoiding the streets in anticipation of her occult retaliation. Yet, within the context of that same story, Elly Kedward single-handedly terrorizes an entire community for three hundred years.

The ability to provoke contradictory reactions in listeners is a defining element in all traditional witch tales, including modern renditions like *The Blair Witch Project*. Portrayed as both victims and culprits, witches refuse to fit neatly into good guy or bad guy stereotypes and, in Elly Kedward, the conventional, paradoxical role of the colonial witch is faithfully re-created. Consider this: despite being unjustly accused, stripped of everything she owned, and turned out to die alone in a blizzard, Elly Kedward is *not,* in any viewer's estimation, a sympathetic character. In a blatantly backward interpretation of justice, the audience is encouraged to believe that actions attributed to the Blair Witch *after* her death somehow justify her original punishment.

Sánchez and Myrick might have been experimenting with their medium and their technique when they began filming *The Blair Witch Project,* but their title character, even if uncast and unseen, remained true to a three-hundred-year-old storytelling tradition, as the following tale reveals.

"The Carlisle Witch," in a variety of forms, is a story that has been traveling around Connecticut for at least eighty years, and was retold, in a considerably abbreviated version, by Jarle Yvanovich at the 1998 Silver Moon Convention, an irregular gathering of professional storytellers. Three other versions, with minor differences, were offered in response, but, while details vary, the essence of this story remains the same and should prove eerily familiar to Blair Witch fans—even if the pages don't jump about or give you motion sickness!

The Carlisle Witch

Ambele Wedge, wife and young mother in the proud new community of Carlisle, greeted October 23, 1795, by trudging through a blanket of fresh snow, the first of the season. With two oaken buckets dangling from her hands by rope handles, she approached the Mill Pond carefully, intent on collecting the first of the day's water without soaking her shoes or her sleeves. With breakfast to prepare, eggs to gather, and the cow to milk before Meeting, she had no time to spare for drying or changing clothes.

A mild reproach against whatever power found it necessary to send winter early this year slipped past her lips as she crouched to break the skim of ice over the shallow end of the pond. She and Hanson, the bright-eyed young man she'd allowed to court her for nearly a year before finally agreeing to marry him, hadn't done poorly this year. They'd brought in enough food to keep them through the previous winter and managed to clear sufficient land to assure them of saleable quantities this time next year. Young Josiah, a miniature replica of his father, would be running through the fields behind them by then and, if God was kind, perhaps this next one would be a girl for her to fuss over.

Caught up in dreams set beyond the dreary winter approaching all too quickly, Ambele's only response to the sudden collapse of the pond's glassy surface beneath her bucket's edge was a slight gasp as she toppled forward. The rest of her breath quickly followed that soft exclamation when first her free hand, then, suddenly entangled in the massed skirts, which had made the walk here comfortably cozy, both feet slid down the snow-slicked embankment. For scant seconds, thin ice held her. Dimly, she heard a precious bucket skitter far out across the ice. Between one breath and the next, lacy fractures formed beneath her. With a single crack, the transparent surface failed.

Icy water forced its way up her nose, down her throat, wrapped itself around her chest, squeezed the last breath from her body. Blackness surrounded her. Up and down disappeared as cold stabbed her from all directions at once. Stomach muscles clenched against swallowed water. A flailing hand skimmed soft mud and moss. Slimy leaves of dead duckweed trailed against parted lips. Bottom. She was on the bottom. Up. She had to get up.

Kicking wildly against her own clothes rising around her, Ambele Wedge fought for a foothold on the spongy underwater floor her hands had found. Unable to get her feet beneath her, she pressed down hard with first one hand, then the other. The back of her head bounced firmly off the surface. She'd floated *under* the ice!

What had appeared so fragile as she lay above it soon proved itself immune to her weakened pounding from below. Darkness was rising around her, the light from above stained purple as each silent effort pulled water deeper into her lungs. Panic forced mute screams between tightly clenched lips as one of her pounding fists stuck fast to the ice above.

Ambele's body curled around the transfixed hand. Feet that had floated freely finally found purchase on moss-covered rocks. Rocks! Abruptly reversing the focus of her fading attention, Ambele Wedge pressed against her frozen hand, using it as a fulcrum upon which the rest of her body might turn as she strained back toward the black bottom. Two fingers brushed the edges of the rocks. The toes of her shoes

found the pond floor. Water streamed across her face as she surrendered any semblance of control over lungs already in revolt to strain another fraction of an inch lower. Fingers closed around a stone, lifted it, and legs already numb beneath the knees lurched upward.

Even as her head followed her hand, breaking the surface, shattered ice cascading over her, Ambele wondered if she could clear the water from her lungs before the lurking blackness pulled her down again. Breathing, a thoughtless action just moments ago, became an exercise of will, each separate motion requiring deliberation, her complete attention.

The morning's pleasant breeze sliced through her as she groped at the edge of her ragged hole. One hand, oozing blood from circular patches where her skin had clung to ice, refused to respond and she cradled it against her chest as her body violently expelled water from stomach and lungs. Her legs were numbed stumps beneath her when she could once again raise her head to gasp cold, sweet air without coughing. Slowly, one-handedly, Ambele Wedge beat against the frozen rim closest to shore until, crawling over ice and rocks, she hauled herself up the bank.

Snow cushioned her frozen figure. Exhaustion tugged her lids lower as her gaze followed the trail of her own footprints toward the path home. From here, she couldn't see the sturdy house Hanson had built for them, but surely he'd miss her soon. Josiah would need her, was probably already fussing for his first feeding. Hanson would come looking for her soon. She'd rest here, for just a moment, she told herself, just until the

Left: "Witches and water go together like peanut butter and jelly," claims oral storyteller Vince Martin. "The Carlisle Witch, the Blair Witch, and almost every other witch story I've ever heard all include at least one bit where there's a witch— or suspected witch—in a pond or a creek. There's probably some underlying symbolism at work there, water associated with the moon, the moon associated with knowledge, and witches associated with inexplicable knowledge."

shivers wracking her body eased enough for her to stand. Soon now. She smiled. Yes, already the shaking was easing. Another few moments, that was all.

Pain poked at her through the darkness. Voices yelled her name across great distances. Rough fingers dug into her shoulders, shaking her until her head snapped back and forth. Her weak protests only provoked her tormentors to further intrusions. She screamed as heat scalded her feet before working its way toward her heart.

The small community gathered for that evening's Meeting was sombre, the fate of Ambele Wedge much on its collective mind. Small knots of folk gathered round the two women who'd just now left the spent young woman wrapped in blankets before her hearth fire. "A near thing . . . She's young, healthy. She'll have other children—though not this spring. . . . A miracle she got out at all." Young mothers spoke hushed warnings to the children they urged even closer to their skirts than usual. The men said little but many hands found their way to Hanson Wedge's shoulder as families filed past him to their own places on the benches around him. So wrapped up were they in the near-tragedy in their midst that, even in this small company, the absence of David and Mary Prowse, along with their daughter, Hope, the Wedges' closest neighbors, went unremarked.

❦   ❦   ❦

Hope's cheeks, still reddened from the repeated slaps with which her father had "tested the truth" of her claims, burned brighter still as she was pushed to her knees before the Elders' bench. So close was she to Able Gantry that she could smell his breath even over the musty scent of the tome being shoved toward her.

"Will you swear upon the Book, girl?" The stiff leather cover filled her field of vision. "Will you swear, knowing the eternal flames of damnation await the foresworn?"

Instead of approval, her swift nod drew only another blow across her shoulders. Her father's voice hissed in her ears. "You must swear it aloud, girl!"

"Yes, Father!"

Again the leather cover, along with Able Gantry's fleshy face, loomed close.

"Put your hand upon the Book and swear to God Himself that you've spoken only the truth."

The Book was big enough to accommodate a score of hands her size, but Hope's hand was steady as she let her palm rest lightly on the cover. "I do so swear." Though Hope's downcast gaze prevented her from seeing the other four Elders rise, the rustle of broadcloth told her they were finished with her, for now.

Able Gantry's voice seemed to float down from the heavens as he stood over her still-kneeling figure to speak to her father. "You'll be wanted as well. Your goodwife also."

"Then Ambele will be Questioned?"

"Did you doubt it?"

"No, no." Her father sighed. "When?"

"Not tomorrow. Not fit business for a Sabbath." Gantry's hand fell to rest on Hope's shoulder, but she didn't look up. "Monday, if Ambele Wedge is able to speak for herself then. The following day if she is not."

Even her father paused. "So soon?"

"The Book says we shall not suffer a witch to live, Prowse." His hand squeezed her shoulder, fingers digging into the flesh. "Or do you doubt your daughter's word after all?"

"She has sworn on the Book, hasn't she?"

"That she has." As the Elder's fingers finally released her, Hope shrank back until her back pressed against her father's legs. "The question is, will Ambele Wedge do likewise?"

Ambele Wedge, wandering in a strange landscape of hot pain, swore nothing that Monday, or Tuesday either, but word of the Questioning spread even in her absence. On the morning of October twenty-eighth, the packed Meeting Hall made the open space surrounding

Hanson Wedge's small family all the more obvious. No consoling hands had gripped his shoulder, or even held open a door this morning as he carried his young wife to her usual place.

Throughout the short morning service, Ambele's responses dragged a half-second behind the rest of the community's, and, when Meeting finally ended, she was the only one to gather up her outside clothes. Hanson's hand caught her wrist as the Elders stood again and Able Gantry pulled a single sheet of paper from the back of the community's Bible.

Gazing out across the faces as if seeing them for the first time, he asked. "Is Ambele Wedge present among us?"

A frown creased her forehead, but the young woman's voice was steady as she answered. "I am here."

"Ambele Wedge, do you recognize the authority of the Council of Elders of Carlisle?"

Like a bird examining a new piece of grain, Ambele's head tipped to one side while she stared up at the five men who made up the Council. "Of course."

"Then you recognize our authority to Question any member of our community?"

"I do."

"And do you also recognize the authority of the Council of Elders to render judgment if one of the community has broken our laws?"

"I do."

"Then you submit yourself freely to the Questioning of this Council and accept its judgments."

"Of course." She turned to Hanson. "What . . . ?" But he refused to meet her gaze and, for the first time, Ambele Wedge seemed to recognize the silence of the crowd around her, the stiff shoulders of those in front of her, the intensity of Able Gantry's gaze. She stared at Hanson. "Me? I'm to be Questioned?"

Before he could answer, Able Gantry shook the sheet of paper he held, drawing her attention back to him. "Come forward, Ambele Wedge, to hear the charge against you."

Hanson's head jerked up but to stare at Gantry, not to meet his wife's gaze. "She can't. She can't walk. Her feet . . ."

Ernest Baker, sitting next to Gantry, laid a hand on his arm before speaking directly to Hanson. "The Questioning is no torture, Hanson Wedge. If your wife cannot stand to hear the charge, you may carry her to a seat here." With his free hand, he motioned for a bench to be cleared and set before the Council.

Ambele Wedge sat alone on the hastily emptied bench as the sheet of paper was read aloud in Able Gantry's best public voice.

"A statement, sworn upon the Book, by Hope Prowse.

"On the morning of October twenty-third, in the year of our Lord seventeen hundred and ninety-five, while approaching the Mill Pond, Hope Prowse, a spinster in the house of David Prowse, her father, did

recognize Mistress Ambele Wedge, her neighbor, carrying buckets for water down the trail to Mill Pond. The morning was clear and cold, allowing sound to carry for some distance and Miss Hope Prowse did hear Mistress Wedge, on seeing the pond was frozen, castigate our Lord with the words, 'Oh, curses! Frozen already!'

"As Miss Prowse watched Mistress Wedge crouch at the side of the pond, there was a loud crash. The ice opened around Mistress Wedge and, before Miss Hope's eyes, Mistress Wedge was swallowed whole into the water! Fearing for her neighbor's life, Miss Prowse dropped her own buckets to run to Mistress Wedge's assistance. Even before she could reach the edge of the pond, however, Miss Prowse realized that the ice had already covered the opening, sealing it as smooth as before!

"Startled by such unnatural happenings, Miss Prowse turned to run back to her own home and fetch her father. Hardly had she determined upon this sensible course of action when, with another mighty crash, she saw Mistress Wedge cast back up from beneath the ice to lie safely upon it and make her own way to shore."

Even before Able Gantry finished speaking, Ambele turned wide eyes to Hope Prowse, who sat between her mother and father, her own gaze fixed firmly on the floor. "You *saw* me fall?" She shook her head slowly. "You saw me and left me to die?"

"The Council will ask the Questions, Mistress Wedge!" Able Gantry leaned forward to catch Ambele's chin in his fingers and guide her gaze back to himself. Satisfied that her attention was once more fixated on the

Council, he waved David Prowse forward to stand before the community, rest his hand upon the Book, and give his testimony.

"Did you witness the events in your daughter's statement?"

"No, Elder Gantry."

"Yet you believe her claims?"

"Yes."

"Why?"

"I saw her running back up the path that morning. She was as scared as I've ever seen her, more scared than when she saw that lynx, more scared than when her mother had to set that arm she broke. She'd left the buckets behind, and her good warm shawl. Hope's a good girl, not given to imagination." He shrugged. "And she swore it on the Book."

Heads throughout the Meeting Hall nodded to themselves. Ambele just stared.

As David Prowse stepped over his neighbor's knees to regain his seat, Ernest Baker picked out a slender figure farther back and waved him to the front. It was Able Gantry, however, who held out the Book.

"You are Peter Grant, owner of the mill at Mill Pond?"

"I am."

"Were you in your mill the morning Mistress Wedge fell into the pond?"

"No, I was already on my way to Meeting. I left William, my boy, to sweep up and follow me, but he didn't see anything either, being inside."

"I saw young William this morning, skipping rocks out onto the ice."

"He likes to play there."

"I imagine he's put quite a few rocks through that ice from time to time."

"Oh, sure. Our third winter there and boys will be idle when they're not told what to do."

"Certainly, they will. I imagine you've seen him make a lot of holes in that ice." Gantry paused. "I imagine those holes take a bit of time to freeze up, likely they give him away when he's playing instead of working."

"I've got to admit, I've caught him idling that way a time or two."

"So, if it takes a small hole like that a while to close over, I'd imagine it'd take a whole lot longer for a hole as big as a woman to close up again, wouldn't it?"

"I'd think so."

"You ever see a hole in that ice close up as fast as Miss Prowse says she saw?"

"No, Elder, I can't say as I have. Fact is, I had to beat the ice away from the wheel that very morning. It still hadn't froze over when I got back from Meeting. Didn't have to clear it again till sometime that afternoon."

"So you'd say it was unnatural for that hole to close up that fast?"

"Yes, I suppose I would."

Even before Peter Grant could make his way back to his bench, Able Gantry called for a startled Jeremiah Clotter to come take his place. The huge hand Jeremiah laid on the Book shook, but he kept his hold on it and met Gantry's eyes. Able nodded and smiled. "Been a while since we've seen you down this way, Jeremiah."

"Business keeps me mostly up Hartford these days, Elder."

"Not being a member of our community, Jeremiah, I'm sure you're a bit confused by all this, you being called for your statement and all."

"Well, Elder, I'll admit to that. I wasn't even here when Mistress Wedge fell into the pond, up around Benton as I recall, so I don't really see how I can help you." Glancing around the packed Meeting Hall, he quickly added, "Not that I'm not willing to help, you understand?"

Able Gantry laid the Book aside and smiled at the itinerant smith. "Don't you worry yourself now, Jeremiah. We aren't looking for information about Mistress Wedge specifically, but, you, being more well traveled than most of us, you've probably heard just about every bit of news there is to hear in these parts, wouldn't you say?"

"People do tend to talk while I'm working on their animals, that's true," Jeremiah agreed. "But, not to the point of idle gossip. Just the local news is all. Who married who last season, who's sick or died. You know, just local news. Sometimes someone will ask about a friend up the road a bit, or ask me where I'm headed next and give me a letter to take along, but that's all!"

Able Gantry laughed as he gripped Jeremiah's shoulder with one hand and slapped his own thigh with the other. "Take it easy, Jeremiah, we're not accusing you, not you of all folk, of *gossiping*. And, even if your tongue *was* a bit free in your mouth, why, you're not one of the community here, Jeremiah. Tisn't *you* we're Questioning." He slapped the big man on the shoulder once more before stepping back to regard the entire room once more. "No, we're just saying a man who travels about as much as you must hear nearly all the news around, that's all, have a fair idea of what's happening all over. Wouldn't you say that's true? That you probably know all the births and all the deaths as happened hereabouts? At least, most of them?"

"Well, sure I do hear a bit." A deep frown drew Jeremiah's brows nearly together as he glanced from Able to Ambele Wedge. "But I didn't hear nothing about Mistress Wedge's accident until after I got here, so I still don't see how I can help."

"Just tell me something, Jeremiah. How many drownings you hear about in the past little while? I'm sure there's been some."

"Why, sure. Always someone unfortunate enough to die that way, even in the summer when the creeks are low."

"But, how many have you heard of in the winter?"

"Oh, least a dozen or so. Frank Tremblett, up Hartford, did drown in the river there just this spring, couple weeks before the ice broke up properly. True Thomas, over Trinity Falls way, drowned in the pond behind his own house two days after Christmas. Little Bertie Chismhold, Peter Chismhold's youngest boy, he died just the week before True in the same pond—" Jeremiah fell silent as Gantry cut off his list with a wave of one hand.

"So, there's lots of people drown in the winter, from little children to grown men who should be well able to fend for themselves?" Clotter nodded. "But, in all of those cases you know about, you ever hear of someone like Mistress Wedge, who survived a drowning?"

Jeremiah Clotter's mouth opened, hung, then closed again. "Why no, not that I can recall, Elder. That's why everyone was so full of that news when I got here, it being so strange. Porter Chismhold, young Bertie's uncle, he survived a good dunking this summer, but, like you said, it was summer. They pulled him out limp and looking half dead, but he wasn't likely to freeze in August! After he spit up a bit, he was just fine."

"So, in all the places your trade takes you, for as long as you've been working these parts, you've *never* heard of anyone who came back out of the water in winter and lived?"

"Well, now that I'm thinking back, no, I can't say as I have."

"Thank you, Mr. Clotter."

Jeremiah watched Able's back as the Elder turned to pick up the Book again. "That's all? That's all you wanted me to say?"

Able Gantry looked almost surprised to see Jeremiah still standing there. Shaking his head, he spared the bigger man another broad smile, another quick clap on the shoulder. "That's it, sir." Glancing out over the crowd, he called, "Is Brother Clement here?"

From the back of the Hall, a stooped man carrying another leather-bound book eased past his neighbors to work his way forward. He'd just drawn even with the retreating Jeremiah when the smith stopped and turned back.

Able Gantry glanced up at him with raised eyebrows. "We're finished with you, Mr. Clotter. Meeting is over, you're free to go back to your work. Mr. Miller's axle rod, wasn't it?"

"Yes, sir." Still he lingered, gaze moving from Ambele's blank face to Gantry's. "It's just, I wouldn't want anyone thinking I know everything about everyone—"

"I think we've already said no one would accuse you of being a common gossip."

"That's not what I mean. I mean . . . I mean, just because I haven't heard of someone making it through a fall like Mistress Wedge's, that doesn't mean they haven't. Could be there was and I just didn't hear about it, that's all I'm saying."

Gantry nodded and waved Brother Clement forward again. "Thank you again, Mr. Clotter. I'm sure Brother Clement here will help make everything clear for the good folk of Carlisle."

The aged man didn't even wait for Gantry to hold out the Book before grasping its edge. "I'm ready, Elder." His swearing was as brisk and steady as his treatment of the lesser book he'd brought. In answer to Gantry's opening questions, Clement confirmed that it was he who had the care of the burial records for not only Carlisle but Brighton and Clearwater, both just down the road. "As they'll be using our burying ground come the spring, they copied the records of the old ones as well, just in case there was ever a question of where a particular individual was actually interred."

"And how far back do those records go?"

"Here, just to 1782, there being no town here before that. Brighton records go back to 1756, Clearwater's to spring of 1740."

"A fair number of people represented in that book then?"

"Fair."

"And, among that many, surely some of them were unfortunate enough to die drowning?"

"Fifty-three."

"Fifty-three?"

"I counted 'em, like you asked."

"Fifty-three."

"Fifty-three."

"And you, Clement, how long you been living among our community?"

"Since '83. Lived in Clearwater my whole life before that."

"And how old will you be this year?"

"Seventy."

"So, you must know a lot of families around here?"

"Most. Not all the young ones, but their mothers and fathers, their grandparents."

"You ever hear of anyone pulling themselves up through ice like Hope Prowse says Ambele Wedge did?"

"Nope, never."

"Not even once."

"Never."

Gantry wandered back and forth a bit, hand rubbing his chin as he thought. Finally, he paused to lean against the wall farthest from Brother

Clement before asking, "You ever hear of *anyone,* maybe a bit further off than Clearwater, even, doing such a thing?"

"Yes."

Silence settled over people who'd begun shifting about.

Able straightened away from the wall. "Really? Who?"

"A woman in Raleigh, don't know her name."

"How'd you come to hear about her?"

"My father married twice, his second wife had family down that way. She told of a woman who was thrown through the ice, into a good deep pond, who came right back up again."

"*Thrown* through the ice, Clement? Is that what you said?" At Clement's curt nod, he continued. "Why would anyone deliberately throw someone onto a frozen pond?"

"They said she was a witch—"

The rest of his statement was lost first in the sudden high keen that burst from the previously silent Ambele, then in the rustle and rising murmur of the crowd around them. It took some time for Able Gantry to make himself heard once again. "A witch?"

Ambele rocked gently back and forth, eyes staring ahead, arms clutched about herself, head shaking back and forth in a continuous negation of each word.

"Yes."

"What purpose was there in throwing this woman, even if she was a witch, into the water?"

"As the Book says, water is the medium of baptism, with water are our sins washed away. God will not suffer a witch to drown, Elder Gantry. Instead He will cast her forth, denying her even that much of His presence."

"And this woman in Raleigh, she *was* a witch?"

"By every test they knew, yes."

"And she didn't drown?"

"No."

"Just as Ambele Wedge didn't drown, when all evidence to the contrary *proves* she ought not to have survived?"

"Just so."

Only Able Gantry's next question, cast out on nothing more than a whisper, kept the community within the Hall silent. "And what happened to this woman in Raleigh?"

"She burned. The water may have refused her, but the flames of Hell welcomed her warmly enough."

Hanson Wedge stumbled to his feet, pressing easily past neighbors who shrank away from him, to stand behind his wife's crouched figure. "You . . . you can't . . ." His mouth continued to move, but no words came out for several seconds. Only when Able Gantry began to speak did Hanson find his voice again. "The Book—the Book says, 'Thou shalt not kill!'" A hesitant glance around him drew no response from his neighbors. "Thou shalt not kill. . . ."

Gantry's hands spread before him. "And here then is the Question this community itself must answer." Turning his back on Hanson and addressing himself only to Ernest Baker and the remaining Elders, he asked, "How do we reconcile that the Book forbids us that ultimate punishment practiced in Raleigh, yet tells us also that we must not permit this witch to live?"

For Ambele Wedge, the remaining hour consisted of little beyond the incessant murmurs assailing her from all sides and a fleeting glimpse of Josiah being carried away, asleep, in the arms of the Gantry household's baby nurse. Her faint "No!" reached only Hanson's ears.

Only Hanson remained to watch the final moments of the Council's verdict played out beneath overcast skies threatening yet another unseasonable snowfall, under clouds so thick, so heavy, that they subdued even Gantry's voice. "Ambele Wedge is cast out from this community. May God Himself judge her."

With nothing but the clothes she'd worn to Meeting, Ambele Wedge hobbled between the frozen figures of her neighbors standing lifeless, scarecrows, outside the Hall. No hand was raised against her; no hand steadied her. To Carlisle, she ceased to exist.

November 1, 1795, All Saints' Day, Samhain

As if Josiah's wails, audible even outside, weren't enough to hurry Hanson along, the shuffling of bovine feet in the byre ahead reminded him once again that he was late to the milking. With no wet nurse willing to suckle the boy, Hanson's mornings now began with the apparently impossible task of filling the child with nothing more than a pan of warm milk and a new-whittled spoon so small it threatened to break each time he scrubbed it.

His breath fogged the air ahead of him. It had been cold overnight, colder than he could ever remember. While Josiah fretted in his crib, Hanson had watched frost etch patterns over their window. He harbored no illusion that Ambele could have made it to Benton yet. Even on whole feet, with the aid of travelers heading east, it would have taken her nearly a week to reach her uncle's home. But Trinity should have been within reach that first day. Just three miles downriver, with a good road between there and here, Trinity, he assured himself, was an attainable goal. His Ambele was no quitter; she'd have made it.

Josiah's cries hit a frantic pitch as his father pushed through the low doorway. Guilt and relief in equal measure surrounded him as he put the heavy door between himself and his son. Under the cow's stern eye, he blew on his hands, kicked the stool into place, and reached for the bucket.

Warm milk lapped up around his fingers as he gripped the lip.

Jerking his hand back only allowed his eyes to confirm what touch had already told him. The bucket was full. Sitting heavily on the stool, he watched the heavy droplets splatter from his fingertips to the floor as shudders wracked him. For days now he'd endured the loneliness, hearing wagons speed up passing his gate, watching the Prowses take the long way around both properties on their way to Meeting, hurrying to Mill Pond before dawn to avoid the eyes of Peter Miller and the boy. Though the Council had claimed no blame should accrue to the witch's husband or son,

Hanson had spoken to no one since the Council's ruling. That someone would lighten his load by even this small measure caught him off guard.

It was only as he took up the bucket, closed the door behind him once again, and began casting about for the possible identity of his unexpected helpmate that he became aware of some missing element. Wisps of his breath still formed clouds around him, the snow still squeaked under his shoes, the sun was still flirting with the horizon, but Josiah was no longer crying.

Even as he quickened his pace he knew who'd drawn the milk.

Bursting into the house, he found Josiah's crib drawn up before the hearth where the pan, only half full, rested beside a still-damp rag that smelled strongly of milk. The small spoon rested where he'd left it on the table.

Gathering his son into his arms, he reached for the rag, dipped it into the pan, then eased it between the boy's lips. Looking nowhere in particular, he spoke to the air itself. "He's all right now, Ambele. Go, now, before the weather worsens, while everyone is at Meeting and there's no one to see you creep away from here."

When the front door closed, Hanson dipped the rag again and again.

November 20, 1795

Jeremiah Clotter's wagon, the irons, his fire, and bellows took up most of the Wedges' yard. Jeremiah himself took up the rest as he organized the tasks to be done according to the heat necessary to complete them, then leaned on the bellows beneath the portable forge. With a head jerk toward the wagon, he said, "I delivered your letter to Benton. There's a note there, in the box under the seat, by way of an answer." He didn't look up from the glowing fire.

16 November 1795

It is with shock and great sadness that we received your letter of 10 November. Though we wish it could be otherwise, we regret to inform you that Ambele has neither arrived nor sent word. Her aunt and I will begin inquiries at the intervening towns, but after so long we can only suspect the worst.

I remain yours,
Josiah Bambridge

November 24, 1795

Able Gantry's wagon, even with a full four pulling, lumbered through the drifts left by the season's first blizzard. For two days, Hanson and Josiah's world had narrowed to house, barn, and byre. Rather than chance the trek to Mill Pond, Hanson had melted snow for their water. To have arrived so early this morning, the Elders must have left town on the storm's coattails. Shading his eyes against the brilliant skies that so often follow the biggest storms, Hanson watched the wagon driver leave the five men to make their own way down while he walked between the horses, bending often to check a leg or hoof.

The Elders, however, had their goal in sight and clearly knew what they intended to do once they arrived. Without speaking among themselves or to Hanson, the two youngest Elders split off from the others, circling left and right around the house, their eyes scanning the snow. The remaining three, nearly shoulder to shoulder despite the difficult footing, bore down on him.

It wasn't just a long ride in the cold that had put color in Able Gantry's face. His voice staggered under the burden of his wrath. "We'll have the witch, Hanson! And you as well if you've sheltered her!"

"Wha—"

Ernest Baker loomed behind Gantry's shoulder. "A wise man weighs his words for truth before he speaks them."

"And William Beckett has already condemned her!" Gantry's gaze shifted between Hanson and the Elders now disappearing behind the house.

"I don't know what you're talking about—"

Baker's raised hand cut Hanson off once more. "Two nights ago, William Beckett was settling his animals under cover when he saw a woman rummaging vegetables in his fields. She ran when he hailed her, and William, calling out to his boys for a lantern, set off after her."

"It was that wife of yours, Wedge, he saw her plainly! And we mean to have her for a thief as well as a witch!" Elder Cooper shook with anger as he pushed his way closer to Hanson. "She'll neither steal nor cast spells without her hands!"

Hanson shook his head slowly, looking from one man to the other. "As God is my judge and my salvation, I have not seen her, then or since."

"And *Beckett* swears, when last he saw her, that she was headed here." Gantry pointed toward the rising sun. "Our Lord knows she'd find no help at the Prowses!"

Hanson's bitter agreement did nothing to divert the Elders from their search. When no tracks were found outside, they invaded the house and outbuildings, rummaging through spaces too small to conceal even a child.

Not one of them spoke a word of farewell before kicking their way back to the wagon.

When Hanson returned to the morning's chores, he didn't rush. He'd no intention of making it to Meeting today or any other day.

November 27, 1795

The flickering of torchlight through their window, the hammering on the door, and the sound of a woman's screams haunted Hanson's dreams so often now that, when a real voice called him in the darkest hours of the morning, he barely stirred.

"Hanson! Hanson! You've got to come! Please, Hanson!"

Only Josiah's startled wail roused him completely. Pulling on his pants, he cast a quick glance through the window, to satisfy himself that the witch-hunting mob of his dreams hadn't descended on his front door, before pulling it open.

The flickering flames didn't come from a hastily constructed torch but were contained within the housing of a simple lantern carried by Mary Prowse. "She's taken Hope! Hanson, please, please, help us find her—"

"Who's taken Hope?"

"Ambele!"

"What?"

Mary's hands shook so hard the lantern nearly fell from her fingers as she gripped the edge of the door. Her voice, a shriek just seconds ago, fell to a whisper. "Ambele, it's *got* to be Ambele."

When the woman swayed to one side, Hanson muttered under his voice and half carried, half pushed her to the bench in front of the hearth. Taking the lantern from her, he set it on the table. His first clear look at her face startled him. Sunken eyes and cracked lips, common enough after a long winter, weren't normal in a woman who should still have the whole of this year's harvest available to her. Surreptitious glances as he stirred the banked fire back to life confirmed the wasted appearance extended to a figure several sizes smaller than the day dress he'd seen her fill just a month before. The fingers curled about one another, while never plump, seemed little more than bone and nail now. When they reached out to grip his arm as he breathed softly over the kindling, Hanson coughed and shuddered.

"You've got to send her away, Hanson." The urgent whisper brushed the side of his neck until he pulled free of the viselike grip. "Please!"

"She's not here, I tell you." Crossing his arms over his chest, he stared down at Mary Prowse's bowed head. "I haven't seen her since the Questioning."

"Neither have we. Seen her, I mean." The eyes she lifted to him were more white than colored. "No one *sees* her! But it's her, I tell you. It's her. And now she's taken my Hope." The gaunt figure rocked slowly. "I didn't mind the vegetables, Hanson, truly I didn't. And I never mentioned the eggs, not even to David. I knew it must be her taking it, but I didn't say so. Hope it was who told me about the wood, before the storm." Her gaze dropped to the fresh splits of dried wood Hanson had dropped into the grate. "I wished her well of it, honestly I did, but nothing appeases her!" Mary Prowse's voice gathered volume once again as her shoulders began to shake. "First the tapping, then the calling, waking us half the night. Scared Hope so bad, but I told her she was safe. . . . I told her she was safe. David's been out there for hours, but we can't find her." Again those wide eyes fixed on his. "You've got to help us. Make her bring Hope back."

Hanson shook his head. "You're mad, woman. Who hasn't lost a few eggs in winter? Or had raccoons find the vegetables?" Backing away from the quaking woman in front of his fire, he glanced toward Josiah. The child had quieted when the knocking stopped, but he still rooted softly under the blankets. "And, I put it to you, Mary Prowse, that if your daughter hears voices accusing her in the dark, it's more likely to be her own conscience than my wife." The rocking stopped abruptly as he reached for the door. "Go back to your own home, Mistress Prowse, and leave me to mine."

She said nothing as she rose to her feet, gathered up her lantern, pulled her sleeves down over the withered hands. In the doorway, she paused to look ahead to the trees between their two properties. Dimly, Hanson could see lanterns moving along the path. Voices, of David Prowse and the neighbors farther down the road, were muffled by yet more snow beginning to fall. "You're wrong, Hanson. I don't know how she's survived, but she's out there, and she's got my daughter." Mary Prowse stepped outside and, before Hanson could close the door, added, "And, if you could hear what we've heard, you'd know it's not me who's mad."

November 28, 1795

For the first time Hanson could remember, there was no morning Meeting in Carlisle's Hall. Instead, the community turned out to search for a young woman who, according to her parents, had gone missing from her own bed the night before. Like everyone else, Hanson Wedge diligently searched his own property for any sign of her, but unlike every other able-bodied man, he steadfastly refused to join the greater search emanating from the Prowse property or to allow anyone else access to his land.

He was walking the tree line around noon when he heard the first shout, off toward Mill Pond, announcing an end to the search. Standing at the edge of his property, he watched as a vacant-eyed Hope was half-carried, half-marched back to her home. When her gaze happened to fall on him, it slid off again with no more concern than it would have had if it encountered yet another tree. Without a word, Hanson settled Josiah deeper inside his coat, turned his back on the crowd of searchers gathering around the girl, and set off for his own home.

At evening Meeting, it was generally agreed that Hope Prowse's silence was preferable to the only other sound anyone had coaxed from her so far, an ear-piercing shriek that didn't change her expression one whit.

November 29, 1795

Hanson Wedge was just heading to Mill Pond for the day's first water when he heard hounds baying. Too dark to sight deer or birds; too light for coon. The sun, not yet touching the horizon, told him all he needed to know about the dogs' likely prey.

His legs pumped as he drove through the drifts, fumbling forward until he reached the creek, turning away from the mill and the Prowse property, following the frantic barking. His eyes picked out the churned snow marking the hunters' route just as he came close enough to separate the sounds of men from dogs.

"She's underground!" It was David Prowse's voice.

"Dig her out!" One of Able Gantry's sons? Peter Miller? Hanson couldn't tell who, couldn't tell how many.

Among the trees, the darkness was deeper. Hanson could as easily have stumbled off the creek bank as into the small circle of men urging on the dogs. It took several moments to realize the dogs were down on the creek while the men stood on the bank above. For the first seconds, as rough hands caught him, kept him from tumbling to the ice below, Hanson could have sworn he heard the dogs clawing their way up through the ground at his feet!

His eyes adjusted to the dimness, but even when he could place each man—it *was* Peter Miller he had heard—his ears couldn't reconcile the yapping of the dogs in their semicircle on the ice with the growling from the ground below.

Miller's sons, the leashes in one hand, shovels in the other, advanced on the bank. "Come out, witch! Come out!"

When Hanson would have lunged forward, Prowse's forearm snaked its way around his throat. "She's shunned, Wedge, no more your wife." The words hissed past his ear. "And she's dangerous!" The big man shook him to catch his attention. Below them, the young men probed the bank with their shovels. "She's dug in like an animal! She's not even human anymore, do you hear me?"

"Leave. Her. Alone." Peter Miller's toughened hands gripped his arm. Prowse leaned back, threatening to choke him if he continued to struggle. "Inno—"

"Maybe in the beginning, Wedge, but no more. What she did to our Hope. . . . She's mad, Hanson, as mad as Ambele!"

The dull *thunk* of spades hitting dirt sounded below.

A muffled scream, a double handful of rocks, and a figure, more tattered scarecrow than woman, erupted all at once from the bank. A dog yipped as stones struck its tender muzzle. Graham, the older of Miller's sons, scrambled backward as the shrieking apparition threw itself at him, lost his footing on the smooth new ice, and fell hard. As Henry, the younger brother, dropped the leashes to take the shovel up in both hands, Hanson shouted a warning to the ragged figure. It was Ambele. Peter's fist caught him squarely across the jaw, staggering him, but Ambele crouched and the sharpened slab of metal whistled past her. Before Hanson's vision could clear completely, he heard Graham's groan and Henry's muttered oath, felt the men holding him upright stiffen, and sensed as much as saw the blur of activity on the ice below.

He fell to one knee as Miller and Prowse deserted him to slither down the slick bank.

"She's killed him!" Henry's wail was nearly lost beneath the renewed baying of the dogs.

Pulling himself forward, Hanson watched as the slender hounds reached the far side, intent on the rapidly disappearing figure crashing through the trees ahead of them. Three men huddled around Graham's still form. Bright splashes of red dotted the ice. Hanson, unsure of his legs, let himself roll down the slope. One dog limped close by, licking first its right forepaw, then Graham's pale face, then the blood freezing between them.

Hanson turned his head away only to find himself staring at the open black hole torn into the bank. On his hands and knees, he crawled closer. Though the shovels had collapsed the front wall, the shape of Ambele's most recent home remained evident. A low but deep hole, which might have begun as a den for some wolverine or fox, had been painstakingly enlarged. A drift of snow didn't completely cover the pile of dirt to one side. Straggling roots had been cut away. Dirty cloth, mostly rags, padded the furthest extreme of the hole and shallow depressions formed crude shelves.

As David Prowse left the Millers to tend to their own while he followed the dogs' obvious path, Hanson crept into Ambele's hidey-hole. A rancid odor rose from the rags. His hesitant rummaging revealed three eggs, a small store of near-rotten root vegetables, frost-bruised mushrooms of a type he'd sometimes seen her add to stews. The little holes in the far wall held only two items, a twist of cloth and a wooden comb. Hanson's fingers felt nothing inside the cloth but, in the light of the rising sun, he caught a glimpse of red gold. A single curl, Josiah's, rested inside.

As his finger caressed the tiny circlet, Hanson closed his eyes. At just eight months old, Josiah's hair was beginning to fill in, just barely long enough to wind once around his father's finger. Ambele had been in the house again, and recently.

Tucking the cloth and comb into his pocket, Hanson crawled back outside just in time to watch David Prowse return. The three dogs' wary distance from the red-faced man told Hanson all he needed to know about that particular hunt. As Hanson found his footing and stood, Graham Miller rolled to his side to lose last night's supper on the ice.

"So he's not dead after all."

Though the youngest Miller came to his feet with his hands balling into fists at his side, no one responded or tried to stop him as he turned and walked away.

Back on his own property, Hanson laid the scrap of cloth atop the gatepost, weighing it down with the comb and a stone. When he passed that way again, only the stone remained.

December 3, 1795

The Elders arrived late that evening. As he watched Gantry's wagon approach, Hanson figured they must have left town just after Meeting. He wasn't surprised when none of the five offered him so much as a "Good evening" before Able pulled a single sheet of paper from inside his coat. Hanson could read as well as, maybe better than, most men, so Able Gantry had no real need to read the missive aloud, but he did anyway, with relish:

> Hanson Wedge, the Council of Elders of Carlisle, after much deliberation, imposes the following fine.
>
> For the succor of a woman lawfully shunned by this community, one-twentieth of every part of this season's crop.
>
> For interfering in the apprehension of a thief, one-twentieth of every part of this season's crop.
>
> For failure to uphold the religious obligations undertaken as a member of the community of Carlisle, one-twentieth of every part of this season's crop.

These fines to be payable within three days.

These fines to be doubled on a second instance of any of these offenses.

For a third instance of any of these offenses, the Council of Elders of Carlisle will deem you no longer a member of this community, taking part in none of a member's privileges and, therefore, revoking the grant of land given you as a member of the community of Carlisle.

He actually smiled as he folded the paper and held it out to Hanson. "Good evening to you, *Brother* Wedge."

December 14, 1795

Gemma Hathaway had no reason to be walking on the rough track that petered out into a game trail mere feet past Hanson Wedge's gate. Her husband's plot of land, worked just a season longer than Hanson's own, stretched along the main road on the far side of town. She had no family down here, no business at the Prowses' or the Millers'. She certainly had no reason to walk past Hanson's gate three times in as many minutes. Settling Josiah in the pen he'd had to assemble to keep the boy out of the grate and out of trouble, Hanson pulled on his jacket and stepped out into a warmish winter morning. Gemma Hathaway stopped at the gate, waited.

"Something I can do for you, Mistress Hathaway?"

The woman nodded, opened her mouth, and closed it. Hanson waited, watched as she went through the open mouth–close mouth routine twice more, then looked about pointedly. "It *was* me you came to see?"

"*She* was in town. Last night." Gemma Hathaway's eyes stared at the snow around their feet as if she'd never seen such a thing before. "Behind the Hall."

Hanson froze. "You saw her?"

A quick nod. "Lots of people did. They didn't hurt her, Hanson." Her hands, deep in her skirts, clenched visibly. "Just drove her off." The woman turned on her heel, staring away into the distance. As she spoke, she wrapped her arms around herself. "It was the most horrible thing. . . . She was so cold. She'd pressed herself up against the wall, there where the chimney juts out. I guess it was warmer in there, out of the wind, with the stove going because of Meeting." Gemma Hathaway's shoulders shook but her voice remained steady. "We . . . We just walked on past her, me and James. We acted like we didn't see her there. The Grants, the Pearsons, most everyone, Hanson, just turned their eyes away, let her be." A deep breath later: "But Brother Clement, he stared at her until she had to look up at him. Then he goes into the Hall, brings back Elder Baker, and he threatens to take her for a thief!" She turned back to him then, confusion written clearly across her face. "They, the Elders, they said we weren't to listen to her, to speak to her, to *see* her! They said she was no more than a tree that had stopped bearing but wasn't worth cutting down. They said we weren't even to speak her name. . . ." Gemma's gaze met his squarely. "But *they* spoke to her, Hanson. They told her to get away, said she was stealing *heat* from the rest of us."

"They didn't try to catch her?"

Another shake of her head. "No, they said it wouldn't be right, to do it on the Lord's Day."

"And she just left?" At Gemma's nod, Hanson pulled his own coat close. "Thank you, for . . . for coming to tell me."

He was turning back to the house when tentative fingers brushed his sleeve. "That's not what I came for, Hanson." Dropping her hold, she backed up until she stood in the main pathway. "I heard them talking, after Meeting."

"About Ambele?" Gemma actually winced as he said the name, before shaking her head. "About me?"

"They mean to have you away from Carlisle, Hanson." Hanson watched her gaze wander toward the Prowses'. "They're writing it up now, today. They say as Amb— They say as she can't pay for her thievery last night, that you'll have to pay. Another twentieth." She turned back to him. "I heard them talking. Brother Clement, Brother Gantry, and some others. They're going to keep making you pay, Hanson. Every time they see her, see any sign of her, they're going to take another twentieth. They know how much you've got put up, know this is only your seed season. They don't care!" Shaking her head again, she stepped forward.

"James heard other things, too. And I've heard the women say so, about Hope Prowse."

"Hope?"

"They're marrying her to Peter Miller's son, Henry."

"Hope? But—"

"And she hasn't spoken a word or lifted a hand, even to wash herself, since that night outdoors. She just sits there!" Gemma walked a few steps away, then back, again and again. "They bring her to Meeting and she just sits, rocking back and forth."

"Then why does Henry want her?"

"He doesn't! He wants the Prowses' place, yours too, the whole section along here." Her skirts swirled as her pacing grew more agitated. "Oh, Hanson, why don't you ever come to town? You'd know all this if you'd just come to Meeting!"

"I can't, Gemma, I won't."

"But, if you'd just come, they couldn't do this! They couldn't, not with you there to speak against it."

"Against what? Hope's wedding?"

"Henry wouldn't be marrying her except they all think she's going to die anyway."

"That doesn't make sense."

"It does! Hanson, it does! They, the Prowses, they need the Millers' help. They say as they can't even sleep at night anymore with Amb— With Ambele's doings! Like someone taking great branches and battering them against the house all night, from all sides at once, that's what Mary says. Except in the morning when they go out to look, there's no marks in the snow!" Stopping abruptly, she turned to Hanson. "Is it her, really? Is it?"

"How could it be?"

"I don't know. I only know that Mary Prowse looks near to dying herself, and David not much better."

"But what's any of that got to do with Hope and Henry?"

"Everyone knows Hope won't live long without constant watching. They got to put food in her mouth and hold her nose to get her to swallow. But the Millers say if Hope marries Henry, they'll take care of the Prowses. The Millers have sons, David Prowse only has Hope."

"So the Prowses are willing to marry Hope off to one of the Millers so they'll have someone to watch the house at night?"

"Yes." The hectic color in Gemma's cheeks began to fade as she stared up at him. Her voice dropped to little more than a whisper. "It's so horrible, Hanson. You've got to know that, once they have Hope married off to Henry, they'll just let her die—in time. They'll let her starve, just like Ambele."

Hanson shivered at the scenario Gemma Hathaway was laying before him. The notion of Henry Miller getting a child on the mindless Hope, of them waiting for that child to seal their deal with the Prowses, then letting the mother go. It was monstrous. That the Prowses must be as aware as Gemma of their daughter's likely fate, and that they were willing to allow it, to let her die, just to gain some measure of protection from *Ambele,* shook his soul.

What could she be doing to dredge up such horror?

Gemma Hathaway's hand clutched his sleeve again. "I know you've no reason to feel anything for Hope Prowse, Hanson, I know that, but, surely you could stop all this? Couldn't you just turn Ambele away? Make her leave?" Her fingers dug into his arm. "Doesn't she understand? There's nothing here for her! They'll never let her come back. Never. She's lost. But Hope Prowse isn't. Not yet!"

Hanson shook his head slowly. "She's not here, Gemma. I swear it."

Gemma's taut little figure sagged. "Then there's nothing you can do? Truly, nothing?"

"Nothing."

Shoving her hands back into her pockets, Gemma looked toward the Prowse place once more. "Then they'll both die."

December 20, 1795, Yule

From somewhere in the trees, she watched. He'd spotted her tracks yesterday evening and prayed for snow to cover them by morning, before the Elders came to collect the latest fine.

"It was the Bellows this time," he called aloud. "A sack of potatoes, eggs, and flour." The light breeze played games with his eyes, rearranging the twigs into faces that quickly faded away. "Is that worth a twentieth of our season, Ambele? Is it?"

Josiah's laughter trickled from the doors of the cow byre, brightening this overcast day. Just inside the doorway, he struggled to free himself from the remains of the hay pile, a pile less than half the size it had been last month.

"Will it be worth it come spring when I've no hay for the cows?" He shook his head. "They'll starve us out too, you know. I can't feed Josiah corncobs!" The hands he rubbed over his face shook. "For God's sake, Ambele. If you ever loved us, go!"

The branches of a white willow at the very edge of the clearing trembled beyond any breeze's touch, then silence ruled.

Without another word, he slipped inside the byre, scooped the remnants of hay into one corner and rescued his son, ruffling his hair to make him laugh again. His fingers grazed the spot where a curl had been cut away and he shivered.

December 25, 1795, Christmas

Hanson stirred the fire, grateful for the brilliant sunshine flooding through the window. Behind him, Josiah squealed his delight at the fanciful shapes dancing across the floor. Chubby fingers passed through the ethereal shapes, enthralling the happy child who continued to reach for them.

Only when Hanson had the fire burning well did he stop to really watch Josiah, and only then did he realize how different these shadows were from the random shadow shapes expected through the tree outside the casement. As he looked up, into the light, he squinted, then gasped.

Four tiny figures, bits of wood twisted into stars and angels, twirled from threads hung over the window. Slowly, half expecting the primitive ornaments to disappear under closer scrutiny, Hanson crept to the window. Outside, all was still. No tracks marked the snow. With one finger, he touched a star. It spun lazily—inside the glass!

The fragile things crumpled in Hanson's shaking hands, becoming no more than alder twigs and dried grass. He was staggering as he pushed his way through the front door. His voice, harsh even to his own ears, roused birds from the nearby trees. "Go away, woman! Go away!" He blundered through the snow, ripping the ornaments to shreds, throwing them in all directions. "Or would you have the child eat *these* for his dinner!" The cold bit into him as he sank to his knees. "For the love of God, woman, leave us what little we still have!"

No sounds answered him.

January 22, 1796

Jeremiah tapped the bucket against the edge of the huge vat, which barely fit inside the lean-to Hanson had built to house it. He sighed and said, "No more, man, no more!"

Hanson's buckets thudded down beside Jeremiah's as both men laughed and slid down to sit in the sunshine with their backs against the warm wood. Inside, Jeremiah's young wife, Ida Anne, squealed almost as loudly as Josiah as the two played "bears" under a quilt before the fire. Jeremiah laughed again before tipping up his bucket to catch a few cold droplets against his tongue.

"Think that'll get you through a few weeks?"

Hanson knocked the side of the vat, smiling at the deep echoes that proved it was almost full. "It had better. I can't be dragging water all winter, not if it gets any colder."

Jeremiah nodded agreement. "I wasn't all that sure we'd be able to break through on this side of the pond. And I'd have hated to cross Peter Miller's property to get to the other side."

"Amen."

The smell of roasted meat floated out with the smoke falling over the edge of the chimney top. The smith sucked in a lungful of the delicious aroma and groaned. "Now I remember why I married that girl."

Hanson rubbed his own stomach before getting back to his feet. "I know I can't remember the last time I smelled anything that good."

From his perch on the ground, Jeremiah peered up at him. "You've never thought of remarrying?"

Hanson paused in his bucket gathering. "I have a wife."

"Not in the eyes of the church. Not in your house. Not in your bed." Jeremiah watched Hanson slowly hanging buckets on their pegs. "Haven't you even thought about it?"

"No."

"For the boy's sake?"

"Josiah is fine."

"For now." Catching Hanson's eye, he added, "Or until some other of your good neighbors decide to blame some shortage on Ambele."

"There's nothing I can do about that."

"Taking a new wife would put a lot of gossip to rest, my friend."

"What gossip? That I still meet my witch-wife under the full of the moon? That I'm so besotted with her that I'd sacrifice everything for her?" Hanson's face flushed as he pressed close to Jeremiah. "God's truth? It's nearly a month since I've seen any trace of her and that's fine with me." He'd have brushed past Jeremiah had not the bigger man blocked the way.

"So, has it come to that now? That you'd wish her dead?"

"To keep a roof over Josiah's head and food on his table? Yes."

January 23, 1796

Hanson dabbed the softest of the rags he'd once used to feed Josiah against the parallel scratches angled across Ida Anne's cheek. "I can't believe she did this."

Jeremiah glanced up before driving the last nail through a stout paling and into the rear door frame. "Has she ever come inside before?"

"Yes, but never to harm, never . . ."

Jeremiah checked the paling across the front door once more before turning his attention to filling and lighting the extra lamp. In the brighter light, the full extent of the damage—to the interior and to Ida Anne—came into focus. The screaming presence that had torn through the darkness inside the small house hadn't lasted more than a few minutes, yet little had escaped her attentions. From Ida Anne alone had she drawn blood, but both men sported dark patches that threatened to swell.

All three froze as what sounded like a scatter of small stones skittered across first one side of the house, then the other. Hanson felt Ida Anne tense under his fingers, but she made no sound. No one asked how Ambele could attack both sides of the house at once, or where she might find loose stones in the midst of winter with the ground frozen. When the rattling stopped, she shifted Josiah's sleeping form higher against her shoulder and idly rubbed his back. "It'll be morning soon." The boy snuggled close, resting his face against the side of her neck. "Bring the cot out here would you, Jeremiah?"

Stepping around the overturned benches and carefully avoiding the fragments of a broken pitcher scattered over nearly half the room, Jeremiah took one of the lamps and headed around the fireplace to the sleeping room beyond. Ida Anne reached up to clasp Hanson's hand and pull it away from her face. "It's fine now, Hanson." She stiffened as a sound, not unlike the clatter of a stick dragged along a picket fence, clattered up one side of the steeply pitched roof and down the other. When it faded away, she held the boy out to his father. "Here, hold him while I clear a spot for the cot and put on the kettle."

Holding the child's warm little body close to his own, Hanson, under Ida Anne's firm touch, found a spot on the hearth. From there, he watched her push the table back to its usual place, sweep the broken crockery to the far corner, and, almost as an afterthought, drape her own shawl across the house's only window. When the strident screams began a few minutes later, she was busy tucking an extra quilt into the cot Jeremiah had set near the fireplace. Her only comment as she transferred Josiah from his father's arms to the cozy cot was, "Children can sleep through almost anything, can't they?"

Sleep for the adults came later, after the sun had risen and the shrieks had faded, after Hanson searched and locked the outbuildings and boarded up the window, after Jeremiah lugged in water and fuel enough for several days, and after Ida Anne retrieved Jeremiah's rifle from the hidden space in their wagon bed. Then, between brief, rotating naps, they watched the frost grow thicker on the door's metal hinges, felt cold creeping through the cracks as the temperature continued to plummet, and waited.

Darkness had barely fallen over the remote home when the hammering began. First at the front door, then the back, then all over the walls, even up on the roof, the furious pounding defied explanation. Stones might take such punishment, but not the flesh of human hands. Worse still were the quieter sounds of nails scrabbling at the doors, the low grunts and growls, the almost words, the damp whimpers. Through it all, Ida Anne sat before the fire rocking Josiah. Jeremiah's hand drifted between his wife's shoulder and the rifle. It was Hanson who, midway through the night, threw himself against the front door, his own poundings a pathetically dim echo of the racket outside.

"Leave us alone!"

The sudden silence left them holding their breath, their ears straining. Even so, they barely heard her sibilant hiss: "Never."

Hours later, when nerves stretched taut were near to breaking, the worst came equally quietly. Wisps of warmth, almost welcome on a night so cold that the grate's heat barely reached the far corners of the room, touched Hanson's face like gentle caresses. When Jeremiah's hand closed on his shoulder, jerking him forward and back to full wakefulness, he suddenly realized that in its unconscious search for warmth, his body had been leaning *away* from the hearth—toward the wall!

Jeremiah shook his shoulder sharply. "Smell it?"

And he did. Smoke. Not the clean smoke from the grate, but a denser, acrid smoke.

Ida Anne was already pulling Josiah back up from his cot. "She's set the house afire."

"No . . ." Hanson stared blankly at the wall. "She wouldn't. . . . Josiah."

Jeremiah checked the rifle once more, then handed it to Ida Anne before grabbing the bucket by the hearth and tossing it to Hanson. "Come on." His last words before prying open the front door and pushing Hanson through were to Ida Anne. "She comes through here, you fire. Hear me?" He didn't wait for her quick nod before hauling the door shut again.

Outside, full darkness still covered everything. Cold knifed into Hanson's lungs with even the most shallow breaths. For a moment, he was blind, but Jeremiah's hand urged him on toward the lean-to. "Hurry!"

The ice over the stored water was thicker than either man had anticipated. Buckets alone couldn't break the icy layer. The smell of smoke grew stronger. As Hanson searched for something heavier, Jeremiah grabbed two buckets from the pegs. "I'll scoop snow on the fire until you can bring water."

It took the weight of a heavy mattock to crack the surface, and more precious seconds to haul enough ice out to allow a bucket free access.

Hanson was hurrying toward the growing blaze when she hit him from out of the shadows.

Shrieks tore from a face he barely recognized. Hands clawed at him, ripping into his clothes, nearly dragging him from his feet. Her wails pierced his ears as she clung to him, teeth seeking some hold. Without thought he swung the bucket, felt it strike home, and watched as water sluiced over the screeching creature. Shock silenced her. Immobile, she watched the water soak into her ragged clothes, drip from her fingertips. The stiff wind that was bringing tears to his eyes cut through her sodden clothes, freezing the damp folds. The eyes she turned to him were round, horrified.

The first soaking had been accidental.

The second was aimed deliberately, striking full against her face and torso.

Without a sound, she fled back into the darkness.

Hanson stood watching until Jeremiah's shouts sent him back to the lean-to, again and again, until both men were satisfied the house was out

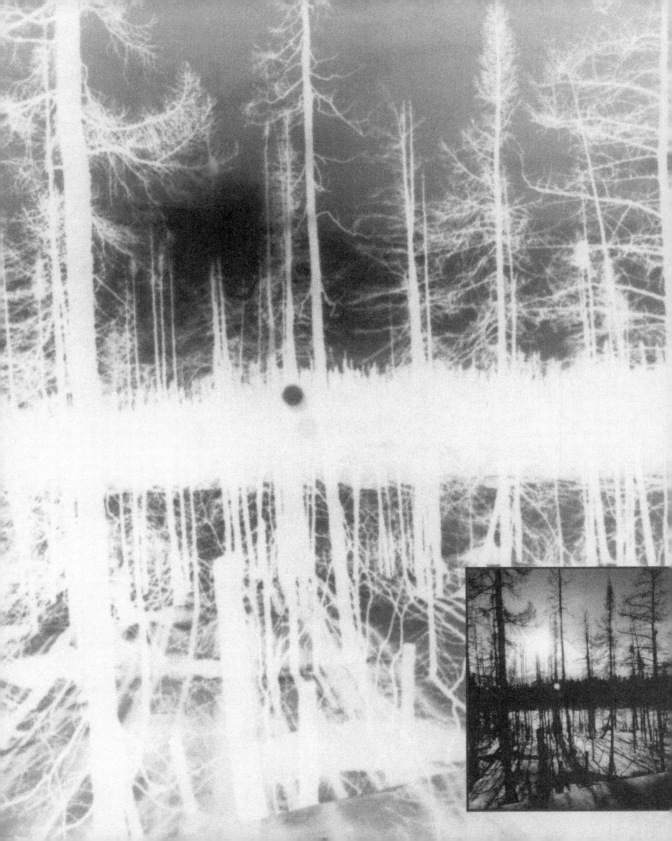

of immediate danger. They shivered as they watched the sky fade from navy to gray. Jeremiah shoved cold hands under his arms as he followed Ambele's trail to the edge of the woods. "No point in following her in there. She won't have gotten far like that. We can have the Millers bring out their dogs."

Hanson shook his head slowly. "No, I'll not do that to her."

Jeremiah frowned down at him. "It would be a kindness, Hanson. Soaked, in this wind, she'll not survive."

"I know."

"So you believe it, then? What they've said about her?"

Hanson's shrug barely disturbed the jacket over his shoulders. "What else could do what she's done?"

January 29, 1796

When the two men returned from a morning's hunt, neither spoke of the other trail they'd found. From the lack of snow in the tracks, they'd recognized the prints as recent, and the blood spatters coloring the snow every few feet gave mute evidence of just whose tracks they must be. They'd followed the trail to the creek. In the shallowest snow, Jeremiah had knelt and traced the awkward outline. "She's barefoot on the left. Looks like she lost toes along with the shoe."

When they reached the side of the mill, saw the handprint where she'd crouched before moving on, saw the spreading stain left behind, Hanson could only shake his head and turn back.

Left: Witches or not, nearly two thousand people get lost in North American forests annually. Most are found within twenty-four hours.

Jeremiah lingered, looking ahead to where the tracks blundered back into the trees, but, eventually, he also turned to retrace his own steps.

January 31, 1796, Imbolc

Ida Anne Clotter answered the pounding on the door shortly after supper, quickly showing Gemma Hathaway to a place near the fire. The woman's face was white with cold. Her teeth chattered as she spoke.

"They've s-s-spotted her again. Outside town after M-m-meeting. They've g-gone after her!"

Hanson stared out the window. "They'll never find her in the dark."

"D-d-dogs. They've got d-dogs."

Jeremiah watched his friend's shoulders tighten and reached for the rifle. "I'm ready."

Leaving the women to watch Josiah and wait, Hanson and Jeremiah bundled up a spare lantern and slipped out.

Gemma Hathaway rocked slowly as she stared into the fire. "B-black. Her nose. Her ears. B-black."

Wrapping her shawl around the shivering woman before stooping to retrieve the kettle from the fire, Ida Anne nodded. "Frostbite does go that way when it goes badly."

They were silent until Gemma had swallowed half the cup of tea Ida Anne pressed on her. "Will Hanson protect her?"

Ida Anne paused in tidying the table. Glancing toward the corner where Jeremiah's rifle had stood all week, she replied, "Whatever else she may or may not be, Ambele Wedge is still his wife. He won't let the dogs have her."

The chase, larger than last time, was easy to locate. Lights bobbed among the trees, and the voices of over two dozen men rose as loudly as the barks of the dogs. As always, Ambele was leading them up Mill Pond Creek. The two men hurried on, cutting along the game trail that brought them out just above the mill. Hanson was opening the shutters on the lantern in preparation for plunging along the high bank when Jeremiah pulled him up short and pointed across the frozen pond.

Hope Prowse, in nothing more than her thin nightgown, stood knee-deep in the snow. Her mother, hardly better clad for the winter, tugged at her daughter, urging her back toward home. Hope ignored her and continued to stare ahead toward the woods.

"Should we help her get the girl home?"

Hanson shook his head. "No. They planted this seed, let them reap it."

With the lights ahead to give them direction and the lantern to keep them from tumbling down the embankment, they easily gained on the party ahead. Jeremiah doused their light before anyone could recognize them, then, as a chorus of shouts and yelps announced the end of the hunt, he handed the rifle to Hanson and pressed ahead, opening a path with his bulk.

At the sharpest turn in the creek, where it grew deep and narrow, dark shapes moved over the white ice. Almost halfway across, a ragged figure limped forward. Her attention never wavered from the far bank, even when she slipped, stumbled, and fell to the ice. As if her fall was some sort of signal, three men let slip the dogs' leashes and the animals coursed ahead of their owners. One by one, the rest of the hunters, all but Jeremiah and Hanson, skidded down the bank and headed across.

As the first dog drew close to its quarry, Hanson planted his feet and pulled the rifle to his shoulder. He saw her mouth open, black against the white skin, as the slavering animal gained. He was sighting along the barrel, aiming for the center of her chest when he watched her fall again. Startled, he looked up, widening his angle of view. Open water encircled the suddenly floundering woman. The dog that had been so anxious to reach her before now floated in the water beside her, scrambling for purchase on the jagged edge.

"Christ!" Jeremiah's hands covered his face.

Again, Hanson pulled the rifle up, sighted.

Before he could fire, she disappeared.

They waited for nearly an hour, the men on the edge of the ice and the two men above on the bank.

"The water is faster there at the bend," Jeremiah remarked softly. "Ice is thinner, probably thinner than anywhere else she's crossed before."

"Probably."

"She couldn't have outrun the dogs."

"No."

Some minutes later, Jeremiah asked, "What are we doing here?"

"Waiting."

Before long, the gnawing cold drove the rest of the men off the ice. At their head, Able Gantry short-stepped his way behind a brace of dogs. He pulled to a halt at the sight of the smith, and peered into the darkness until he recognized the smaller man for Hanson. He smiled. "Well, Wedge, it seems your witch-wife will trouble us no more."

Hanson's head tipped to one side. "Witch? You still claim her as a witch, Gantry?"

The Elder laughed. "And you still deny it? After she's turned on you as well as us?"

Shrugging, Hanson pointed back toward the river and lifted his voice. "You condemned her because she could not drown. What say you now?"

Hanson and Jeremiah turned to retrace their steps. They heard silence fall behind them.

Just in case this tale, like *The Blair Witch Project,* seems all too familiar to let you pass it off as a complete fiction, you may like to know:

- The community of Carlisle was a thriving group of homesteaders in 1795.

- The community "roll," which was the list of residents for 1795, included "Hanson Wedge, farmer; Ambele Wedge, wife; and Josiah, infant."

- On October 28, 1795, a "young woman of Carlisle" was reported in the Clearwater broadsides to "have survived a fall into Mill Pond." Those same precursors to newspapers would later list a "Mistress Wedge of Carlisle township" as a known thief being sought by local authorities.

- The following fall, when the community rolls were updated, the Wedges are recorded as "Hanson Wedge, farmer; Josiah Wedge, son." Ambele Wedge's name is *not* listed among that year's death roll.

- A Benton circular from February 1796 mentions, almost in passing, the death of "a Carlisle woman" who "drowned on the Mill River."

Scary, huh?

If it's scary for those on the outside, how much more frightening must it be for those who used to be on the inside? While few tales, and fewer first-person historical accounts of the fate of the shunned, have survived from the colonial period, even as oral record, one surprising insight into that act of isolation was provided as recently as 1994. Though formal shunning has, for the most part, gone the way of the pillory as a social deterrent, a few religious groups continue the practice, specifically some among the Amish and Jehovah's Witnesses. One former Witness, who claims to have been shunned by her faith, her husband, and her parents for reading New Age texts and defending many of the precepts of Wicca and other neo-pagan beliefs, wrote this poem as a sort of open letter to her former church. It has appeared on several Internet sites, especially those owned and published by other former Witnesses.

The Shunned

In hiding me,
You've exposed the dark part of yourselves,
All that you've hidden, your worst will.
Yet my human pulse is throbbing still,
Your fear a sure strength with me endows,
In spite of all your fine faith disavows.
My heart, my soul, the craft nor skill,
Cannot touch me, harm me, break me, kill,
Though years settle heavier on my brows.

Whether or not you see me, hear me, feel,
Now and again you'll know my name,
Feel that finger of pointing shame,
In emptiness your souls you reveal,
On your books made altars where you kneel,
You've consecrated flickers, not the flame.

Not surprisingly, perhaps, and despite the fact that the poet wasn't herself a Wiccan, the poem has been adopted as something of an anthem by several neo-pagan groups, including the Golden Coven of New Hampshire, whose newsletter's readership edged just over 16,000 in 1999. Says Shannon Cox, editor, "That particular piece, while an anachronism in time, probably re-creates more closely the plight of those colonial women who were accused, usually falsely, than anything written at the time. It's certainly a reminder that the sort of prejudice and misassumption of authority that marked that era isn't completely dead yet."

# of stickmen, corn dolls, and poppets

Although *The Blair Witch Project*'s stickman was the first totem doll to make it big on the jewelry market—stickman pins, earrings, and amulets were de rigueur accessories for Halloween 1999—variations on that image have been integral to witching tales as far back as 1410. Unlike brooms and tall hats—neither of which, thankfully, were pulled out of the closet for inclusion in the Blair Witch mythos—stickmen, the generic term for anything

Right: The tradi-
tional voodoo
doll, complete
with pins and a
bag to hold some
intimate token
of the victim, is
perhaps the best-
known example
of a "sympathetic
ritual" tool.

intended to resemble the human figure and act as a magical implement, have long been symbolic of magical practice instead of magical people.

Asked to explain how magic works, most occult practitioners will describe a worldview where everything, living or not, is connected. Some ancient civilizations personified the entire planet, calling it Gaia and making every creature and stone a part of her body; many modern-day neo-pagans embrace a sentient form of environmentalism, amalgamating contemporary ecological practice with nature worship; Yoda called it "the Force." In each scenario, the basic law of physics in which every action causes an equal and opposite reaction is taken to another level: the *meta*physical, the occult.

The alignment of stars, reflecting events here on earth, is the underlying principle of astrological readings. The Tarot, *I Ching,* and dozens of other divinatory arts propose that cards, stones, or coins can fall in recognizable patterns when influenced by circumstances or people not directly in contact with the objects being read. This cause-and-effect take on occultism is generally known as "sympathetic" magic. That's not to imply that practitioners of these arts are good, evil, or indifferent, simply that a set of symbols is somehow linked to the events, objects, or people they are believed to portray, that affecting the symbol can also affect the real object. As most magic involves people, it's hardly surprising, then, that human figures in the form of stickmen would play important roles in this form of magic.

Perhaps the best known sympathetic ritual is the sticking of pins into Haitian voodoo dolls in the hope of inflicting injury on the person the

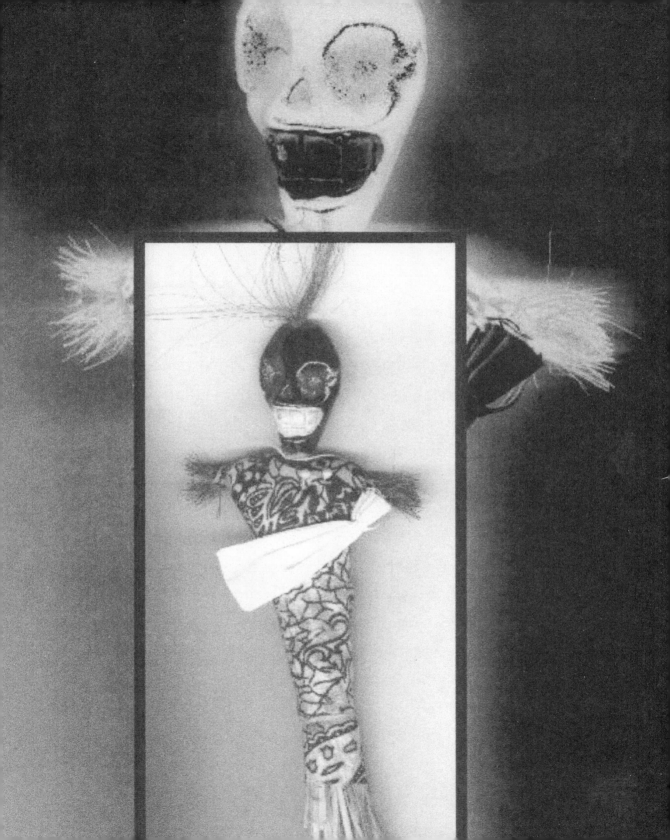

doll is believed to represent. However, that's hardly the extent of sympathetic magical rituals and stickmen. Many such invocations are intended to be beneficial. In China, it was believed that many types of healing could be achieved through stickmen. A barren woman might make a wax figure, a rude self-portrait, to set in the full moon's light while she made love with her husband. As the moon was a fertility symbol, the intent of the ritual was to heighten the woman's fertility through her association with the wax figure. An *iridi,* a crude doll figure dressed in scraps of a specific person's clothes, was the only tool an Iczeki shaman needed to diagnose and treat illness. Distance was no object and, by bringing the doll instead of the actual patient, the family could spare the invalid an arduous trip. Prying open the stick figure provided by the family, the shaman could analyze the way fibers lay within the twigs, note spots of blight or insect damage, and recognize from the natural twists in the stems whether the illness would be chronic or transitory. Then, without stirring from her own home, the shaman could prescribe the regimen of foods, medicines, and prayers necessary to effect a cure.

An even more esoteric use of the stickman was once commonly practiced in Wales. The withe-man, a figure of marsh grass and twigs, built by a young woman while thinking of her intended husband, was believed to draw that young man to her—even if she'd never seen any such living man. The second piece in this chapter, "The Withe-Wife," explores this ritual form of binding more closely. Prior to the release of *The Blair*

Witch Project, stick figures were known to draw people to particular places, and to hold them against their wills.

In England, stickmen were traditionally known as poppets. Like the *iridi* and the withe-man, these dolls could never be confused with children's toys. They were as serious a tool as an adze or a saw was to a carpenter. Unlike the stickmen already described, which usually existed for a short period of time or for a singular purpose, the English poppet, in the hands of a wise woman, might enjoy a very long life and be put to a variety of uses during that time. Some poppets were "born" as infant figures prepared by loving mothers, sisters, or aunts. Infused with the "resonance" of an individual by daubing it with a drop of blood, or by wrapping the figure in the membranes of the placenta (often called caulwrapped), or by affixing a swatch of hair to it, the poppet was then set carefully in a model-sized blanket or cradle. As the child grew, the poppet grew with it, being reformed every so often and updated with new bits of hair or the inclusion of a child's first lost baby tooth. In some cases, the poppet had its own "house," a tiny box that held mementos of the person to whom it was attached as well as the doll itself.

The purpose of such elaborate preparations?

To protect or improve the life of the real person.

If a child was lost, the poppet would lead searchers in the right direction. If the child was ill, treating the poppet would reenforce the treatment given the child. If the winter was cold, the poppets might lie beside the fire to keep children warm while they worked or played outside. If the child suffered from nightmares, hanging the poppet over the sleeping area would confuse evil and the nightmares would bedevil someone else, someone without a poppet.

When settlers from Europe arrived in America, stickman legends and rituals came with them and were adapted to the new environment. In Pennsylvania, the corn doll, a cross between poppets and Native American totem figures, retained many of the poppet's healing aspects, but, unlike the European dolls, this one was given to the children themselves. It was then up to the child to better his or her life by treating the doll as a living being—an esoteric version of the eggs given out as surrogate babies in modern sex ed classes. "Pennyweight" dolls, built from small lead weights used in fishnet knitting, not pennies, accompanied many mariners to sea in the belief that sacrificing the doll during a storm could keep the man himself from drowning.

Of course, not all New World dolls were built with such beneficent purposes in mind. Just as Judaic golems, usually made from mud, were invoked to wreak vengeance—preferably long, drawn out, bloody vengeance—on the enemies of Jews living in Prague's ghetto during the medieval era, many American stickmen were constructed with the full and sole intention of bringing real harm to their namesake. The American curse-doll, usually a clay figure with the real person's name either scratched into its surface or written inside a piece of paper that was then wrapped around the doll, functioned much as the Haitian voodoo doll. In fact, the pin through its heart was often baked right in instead of being applied later. The Dado doll, once found all the way from Louisiana to Oklahoma and Arkansas, was carved from carrots or potatoes or whatever other vegetable was sufficiently convenient and ripe, then julienned as its maker recited the name of her enemy.

With the stickman rituals so prevalent in America as a whole it's not surprising, then, that New England, the conduit for most settlers, should have a rich history of doll legends or that those legends would continue to link dolls and the occult. Haunted dolls, animated dolls, dolls that whisper in children's ears, dolls of all sorts people the ghost and witch tales of present-day Massachusetts, Vermont, and especially Maine. When Maine's best-known writer of horror, Stephen King, scripted an episode of *The X-Files,* the entire story turned on the appearance of—what else?—a doll.

The next two tales incorporate many traditional stickman motifs but, like *The Blair Witch Project's* eldritch dolls, the common focus in both stories is the doll's less well-known ability to confuse and cloud, to tweak perception of the real world.

The Doll House

Hazelwood, July 29, 1949

Dorrie Mercer shook off her sister's grubby grip, reached up high, and pulled herself even with the windowsill. The screening was rusty, the glass dirty, and the interior so dark she could barely pick out the massive white shape of the old wringer washer propped in the far corner of the summer kitchen. The real objects of her scrutiny, dangling high in the shadowy rafters, were visible more for the dim shadows they cast than for themselves.

"Gonna get in trouble, Dorrie!"

"Not if you shut up!" Pushing the seven-year-old aside, Dorrie hitched herself higher, resting both forearms on the sill, to press closer to the glass. "You're just scared."

"I want to go home!"

"Then go, who's stopping you?" A break in the clouds scudding overhead shed brief light through the windows. "Look! Look, there they are!" Forgetting that she'd just told her sister to leave, she let herself down quickly and hoisted the smaller girl high enough to peek inside. "See 'em?"

"Dolls!" Margie's hands, which had been clutching Dorrie's tight blond curls just a second ago, reached for the windowsill. "Hundreds of 'em . . ."

"Well, dozens anyway." Putting Margie down when the child insisted on clinging to the window ledge was almost as hard as holding her up. Both girls were left picking splinters and old paint from their clothes as they huddled close to the wall and contemplated the wealth of toys they'd just glimpsed. "And, it's not like anyone lives here anymore."

"How come?"

"I don't know, but they don't."

"Why'd they leave all their dolls?"

"Who cares, Margie?" Dorrie's gaze wandered along the wall. There were two doors to the summer kitchen, one on this side, a narrower one on the opposite side, the side facing away from the main house. This door was locked with a padlock that was so rusty Dorrie was sure no key could ever get inside it again. The back door, though, had been barred from the inside; she'd seen the piece of wood through the narrow space between the skinny door and the frame. Dragging Margie along in her wake, Dorrie forged ahead through waist-high grass and weeds. The date stone they passed on the corner read 1817. "Thing is, there's no one here now, and it'd be a waste to let them just hang there, getting dirty."

Arguments about "waste" and "cleanliness" sounded vaguely reasonable to Margie, coming as they usually did from adults intent on ensuring that the girls indulged little of the first item and a great deal in the second. Dorrie had her all the way to the back door before she pulled back.

"But we can't take 'em, Dorrie! That's stealing. Momma would kill us for sure!"

Dorrie sighed aloud as she began poking through the usual assortment of garden junk found near any outbuilding. "I'm not *taking* 'em any-where." A smile lit her face as she pulled a thin strip of wood from a tangle of weeds and broken plant lattice and hurried to slip it into the crack. "If we just play with them here, it ain't stealing."

Before Margie could figure out whether or not that was true, Dorrie's first break-and-enter was finished. The door swung open on squeaky hinges, almost begging them to come inside. When Margie hesitated, Dorrie sighed again and shoved her in.

For a moment, both girls just stood there. The view through the window, showing only a part of the room, and through a thick coat of grime at that, had hidden as much as it revealed. Here, inside, they could see the full extent of their treasure. Margie's eyes widened as she took in the rafter's full array. Everywhere she looked, a crude face peeked out between bunches of dusty flowers hanging upside down. Margie couldn't count to ninety-nine, but she knew it was a lot. "They must've had a *bunch* of kids."

Dorrie, full of eleven-year-old wisdom, shook her head until her curls bounced. "Nope, they didn't have any. Poppa says it was only one old woman living here back when. He don't remember there ever being any kids here."

Ever the practical one, Margie was the first to ask, "How we going to get them down?"

The Potters' summer kitchen might not have been used in a long time, but it had been tidied away neatly enough by someone. A long counter with a dry sink stood to one side, another counter with two deep enamel sinks and a pump head between them took up the far wall. A butcher-block table stood squarely beneath the window. Absolutely nothing stood on any of these work surfaces. The cupboards under the counters might hold almost anything, but certainly nothing long enough to reach that far overhead. The old washer, a bench, a broom, a stack of ceramic plant pots, and what looked like a cheap barbeque grill took up the remaining corner. Even if they could move the table or the washer and stand on top of them, they still wouldn't be able to reach the dolls overhead.

Undaunted, Dorrie turned back to the skinny door. "Betcha there's a ladder out back of the garage! Everybody's got a ladder."

"Wait!"

"What for?"

"Don't leave me here!"

Dorrie frowned. "Why not? No one can see you. I'm only gonna be a minute."

"Please?"

"Don't you start crying on me, Margie, I mean it!" Glancing around once more, she nipped into the corner and came back with the broom, an odd-looking old thing, a branch really, with one end split over and over into slender strips. One of her mother's expressions, "a birch broom in the fits"—usually trotted out when her mother was tackling Dorrie's curls—suddenly made sense. "Here, pretend you're playing house." Her hand waved vaguely over the floor. "You can sweep up all this dust while I go look. I won't be but a minute."

Dorrie was gone before Margie could complain. Lacking any better plan, the younger girl did as she was told. Soon, however, it was curiosity, not fear, that kept her pushing dust toward the door. Instead of the plain, grainy old floor she'd expected, a riot of swirling color, grand arcs and tight spirals, emerged behind the old broom. Following a line of purest white, Margie found herself twirling about in a circle half as big as the whole room! Stars and squiggles filled the space inside the circle. Outside, brilliant reds and greens, a yellow brighter than fresh lemons, and a blue like the sky just after sunset, traced mysterious letters that looked nothing like the ones she'd struggled so hard to copy from the banner over the blackboard in her classroom.

She was sitting in the center of the biggest star, the one inside the circle, tracing a green letter that looked like an *M* but had a tiny arrow dangling beneath the last hump, when Dorrie finally returned. "Look, Dorrie!" Like Dorrie could do anything except stare at the startling display. Margie pointed to the line of letters running around the edge, the ones with the flecks of gold paint that made them sparkle even on an overcast day like today. "What's it say?"

Frowning, Dorrie dropped the end of the ladder she'd been about to shove in to Margie, crawled over it, and stared. "I don't know."

It was Margie's turn to frown. "But you did joined-up handwriting in school!"

"I know. I was the one did it, remember?" So caught up was she in the shiny words that she forgot to add the usual smidgen of scorn to her comment. She crouched down beside the smaller girl to run her fingers over the bright letters. "This ain't even in English."

Margie's eyes widened. "It's not? What is it, then? French?"

"Probably." A quick glance around, however, told her that none of the six words she could remember from French class were written here.

"Imp . . . imper-something or other." She tried sounding out the letters, but they made no sense, especially when she came to the letters in blue, the ones that didn't even belong in the alphabet!

"Was the Potters French?" Margie sounded doubtful.

"No, they were American, like us." Dorrie walked around the circle twice, but finding nothing she could read, quickly turned her attention back to the end of the ladder still sticking in through the back door. "Come on, let's get it inside."

It only took a few seconds to haul the ladder inside and determine it would easily reach the dolls up above. It took considerably longer for the two to divest it of the grass and weeds Dorrie had dragged along with it on the trip back to the summer kitchen. Margie, having discovered the beautiful floor, wasn't going to have it dirtied up again. So, while she carefully swept all the debris back out the door, it was Dorrie who stuck the ladder upright in the middle of the room, almost dead center in the big circle, Dorrie who swarmed up the ladder first, and Dorrie who was the first one to reach the dolls. They were everywhere, even more than they'd seen from the floor!

Some dangled from the rafters by bits of yarn, others hid among the closely tied flowers, still more sat atop the rafters themselves. Some were beautiful, some were crude to ugly. One doll, no taller than Dorrie's hand, had a porcelain face with brilliant blue eyes, a shiny green dress, and real hair as soft and blond as Dorrie's. Next to it, another doll, nothing more than a bunch of twigs, would hardly have been called a doll if not for scraps of moss that might be clothes and a swirl of red yarn at the top that might have been meant to be hair. Glancing down at her sister's upturned face, surrounded by real red hair, Dorrie named the doll Margie and tossed it down to her sister. "Here, she looks like you."

"Dorrie, it's ugly! I want a pretty one!" Tossing the doll to the floor, Margie started up the ladder.

"Go back down!" The ladder jerked under Dorrie's hands. "You're going to knock us over!"

"Then give me a nice one!"

Muttering under her breath that she didn't *have* to give her either doll at all, that she didn't *have* to even show her the toys in the summer house, Dorrie reluctantly handed down the figure with the soft blond hair. "Here then, now get down, before we fall down."

Holding the doll in one hand made it harder to climb down, harder to avoid the splinters in the weather-beaten ladder. Delighted though she was by the beautiful doll, Margie dropped it to the floor below in order to get down safely herself. Even so, she didn't see a particularly long splinter until it was firmly embedded in her palm.

"Ow!"

Looking down between her feet and through the rungs of the ladder, Dorrie could see only the top of Margie's head. "What?"

"I got a splinter and I can't get it out."

"I knew I shouldn't have brought you." Urging her sister down to the floor by the simple expedient of threatening to step on her other hand,

Dorrie reluctantly put off further exploration of the doll collection to examine the injured hand.

It didn't look too bad. Sure, it was an ugly big splinter, but there was still some sticking out of the skin. "We won't have to dig it out with a needle," she assured Margie before sitting and pulling her down beside her. When Margie tried to curl her fingers around the splinter, Dorrie smacked them lightly. "I said we *won't* have to dig it out. Stay still a minute and it'll be done."

"I don't want to look!"

"So, don't look." Dorrie tipped her head toward the dolls. "Play with them while I do this."

Dorrie's first attempt didn't work out so well. Margie jerked just when Dorrie had got ahold of the splinter. Instead of sliding out nice and easy, the splinter ripped through the edge of the skin. Blood welled up and Margie squealed. She squealed even louder when Dorrie, ignoring her protests, pried open the fingers she'd reflexively closed and, with a quick yank, finished the job.

"That hurt!"

"It wouldn't have, if you hadn't moved."

Blood speckled the front of Margie's dress and Dorrie's sleeve. The dolls, too, were smeared and more drops continued to well up and drip to the floor. Margie's lip quivered when Dorrie tugged the dolls out of her grip. "You said I could have them."

"Yes, but you're getting blood all over them, and they're getting dust all over you. You want that to get infected?" She pulled Margie's tight fist back into the light and started to peel open her fingers one by one. "Come on, let me look."

"Infected?" There was another of those words that usually came only from adults. Opening her hand to Dorrie's inspection, Margie found the courage to have a look herself. "It's stopping."

It was, but the ragged little hole still didn't look that good. Infection was a word accompanied by enough adult frowns that Dorrie, even at eleven, was reasonably sure it was more of a threat than the boogeyman. How long did it take something to get infected? She didn't know. Was that stingy stuff really the only way to keep something from getting infected? She didn't know. "I think I better take you home."

"But the dolls!"

"We can come back tomorrow—if you don't spill the beans."

Margie stared at her palm. "Mom's gonna ask how I did it."

"So, tell her you got a splinter. Just don't tell her *where,* stupid."

While Margie wiped the rest of the blood off her hand with her clean hand, making things look even worse, Dorrie picked up the two dolls. "I'll put these back before we go."

"Can't we take them with us?"

"Then it really would be stealing."

"Not if we bring them back tomorrow." Margie fingered the stick doll. "I could wash it off before you put it back." With a quick frown, she added, "It doesn't look like me at all."

"I just meant it had red hair."

"Oh." She pointed at the other doll. "And that one looks like you."

"Sort of."

"So, can we take 'em home? Just to wash and bring right back?"

"All right, but don't let Mom see them."

While Margie picked idly at the scab forming on her palm, Dorrie shoved the dolls inside her shirtwaist, wiggling them around to the small of her back.

"You can still see 'em."

More wiggling.

Margie giggled, "There's an arm sticking out!"

It was cool inside the shadowy room, but by the time Dorrie had arranged the dolls to Margie's satisfaction, sweat was beginning to make her hair cling to her forehead. She pushed it back with one hand, blowing the last stray piece aside with a burst of air from the corner of her mouth. Eyeing the ladder, she sighed, "I can't leave that there, can I? Someone might see it. Here, help me put it back."

Getting it down, without bashing it off the rafters and toppling the doll collection, was harder than putting it up, especially with Margie holding her injured hand as far from the ladder as she could. When another stick doll, this one covered in bark clothes, tumbled down, Dorrie was happy enough to take over the ladder herself, sending the little girl to play with the new doll while she wrestled the ladder out the back door and dragged it back behind the garage. She was more than ready to go home when she returned to find Margie sitting in the light from the window, the doll picked to pieces in her lap!

"Margie! What did you do?"

"Nothing! It just fell apart!"

"Right. All by itself." Muttering under her breath, Dorrie thumped down on her knees next to her sister. "Give it here."

The doll, one of the simplest there, nothing more than sticks tied together with bright red string and covered in silvery bark clothes, wasn't hard to mend. Dorrie had the figure back together in just a few minutes and was holding out a hand for the clothes when Margie backed off, using the light from the window to peer inside the crude dress. "Oh, give it to me! Mom's going to be mad enough about your hand without us being late home too."

"There's something written in here." Forgetting herself, Margie used both hands to quickly pick apart the two pieces of bark.

"Margie!"

"Look, it's joined-up handwriting, see?"

It was. A bit faded, but readable. "Allen . . . no, Ellen. Ellen Potter."

"I thought you said there weren't any children lived here."

"There weren't."

"Then who's Ellen Potter?"

"I don't know. Maybe she made the dolls." Seeing nothing else written on the other piece, Dorrie quickly shoved the yarn through the holes in the bark and slipped them back on the stick doll, which she left on the counter. "Come on. We're going to be late."

Mom was mad about the cut, and their tardiness, and the mess of dust and grass stains dotting their clothes, but she didn't ask where they'd been. Being sent to change into something clean while Margie's hand was tended gave Dorrie the perfect opportunity to slip the dolls under her pillows.

Minutes after being tucked in for the night, the girls were huddled on the floor between their twin beds, dancing the dolls around one another in the moonlight. Margie was the first to get bored, the first to remember the name inside the other doll, and the first to begin looking for a similar mark on her own doll. The moss tied around her doll's "waist"—the spot where four sticks crossed—clung to the sticks, Margie's fingers, whatever was handy, so, while Margie fumbled with the stick doll, it was Dorrie who actually found the next marking. Her doll, a piece of stuffed muslin topped with a porcelain head, wore regular cloth clothes that slipped off easily instead of snagging. "There's something written here!" Dorrie whispered before crawling up on her bed to hold the words up to the light.

Abandoning her own doll, Margie clambered up beside her, standing on tiptoe to see the ink scribbled across the muslin fabric. "I know that!"

And she did, having seen Dorrie painstakingly repeat the same swirls and dips all last year. "That's *your* name!" Jumping down to the floor once more, Margie scooped up the stick doll and pulled the moss away in handfuls. "And look! It's me!" Carved in tiny but perfect letters along one smooth twig was, *Margaret Anne Mercer.* "All my names! Thanks, Dorrie!" Margie's excitement turned to a wail of dismay when Dorrie snatched the doll away. "Give it back!"

"Shh! They'll hear you!" Hauling her sister with her, Dorrie crawled under the covers and laid the dolls on her pillow, hissing, *"I* didn't do it, didn't put the names on."

Margie frowned. "It wasn't me. I can't do joined-up handwriting, you know I can't!"

"I know." Dorrie was eyeing the dolls the same way her mother looked at moldy bread.

"Dorrie?" Without another word, Dorrie slipped out of bed and began rummaging through the hamper for the clothes she'd worn that day. When she reached under the bed to pull out her shoes, Margie tapped her on the back of her head. "What are you doing?"

"I'm taking them back."

"What?! No!"

"There's something . . . there's something wrong with them."

"No." Margie snatched up the sticks and moss and yarn, twisting the doll's skirt back around the twigs, forming big loops to make a double bow with the string. "She's mine."

"No, she's not, and she's going back!" Dorrie snatched the tiny doll away before Margie could finish the bow and shoved it inside her shirtwaist. When Margie opened her mouth to yell, Dorrie clamped her hand over it. "Shut up or I'll tell how you helped steal it."

As Dorrie finished tying her shoes, Margie sulked. "Well, what about yours?"

"It's going back too." Suiting actions to words, Dorrie grabbed up the doll and shoved it in her shirtwaist with her sister's. "Now be quiet. I won't be gone long."

"No!" In a flurry of sheets and clothes, Margie was out of bed and falling into her own clothes. "I'm coming too."

The back stairs had never seemed so creaky or the yard so big and empty as it did that night. Half a dozen times they froze as some sound startled them. And, despite the heat all day, they were cold long before they found their way to the fence separating the abandoned Potter place from their own neat yard. The waist-high grass on the far side of the fence whistled as a breeze stroked it. For several minutes, the girls crouched among the bushes just inside the Potter property, caught between the suddenly spooky expanse of overgrown garden and the close-clipped, but too open, lawn they'd just left. Then Dorrie took Margie's hand and dragged her through the bushes toward the summer kitchen, which they could just make out in the moonlight. "Come on. We've got to get back before they go to bed and check on us."

Margie made it to the kitchen's back door with only the occasional whimper but absolutely refused to go deeper into the property in search of the ladder. Finally, Dorrie gave in. "We'll just put them inside, then."

The bright painting on the floor was hidden now. The rafters above showed nothing but blackness, which could as easily have been sky if not for the lack of stars. The old washer was the only relief from the darkness, a patch of dirty gray in the corner. Neither girl moved beyond the doorway. The wonderful playhouse of the afternoon yawned like some animal's cave at night. Holding the door open to admit what little light there was, Dorrie fumbled inside her clothes until she found the dolls, then tossed them toward the nearest counter. She thought they landed in the dry sink but couldn't be sure. Wishing she could somehow bar the door behind them once again, Dorrie took Margie's hand and plunged back into the tall grass.

"Dorrie, I'm scared!"

"Then you shouldn't have come." Yanking harder than she really needed to, she pulled Margie with her. She thought she could hear the muted sound of the radio just ahead. Her folks must have opened the window to let out the daytime heat. Dropping her voice, she whispered, "And, if we get caught, you just say we left that new doll of yours outside. We came out to get it so we wouldn't get in trouble if they saw it tomorrow morning."

"But I didn't take it outside!"

"I know." Dorrie sighed as she looked ahead for the bushes that would tell her they were halfway home. "But when we say we didn't find it, they'll be mad, right?" Margie nodded. "And when we really find it, in our room, they'll be happy and it'll all blow over. Get it?"

A rustling in the grass directly ahead of them brought Dorrie up short. Margie squeezed tight behind her back. "What's that?" A squeal hovered around the words and Dorrie wrapped an arm around Margie to keep her quiet while they listened.

"Nothing. Probably a cat or something. Come on." When she looked up, it seemed the bushes were even farther off than she'd thought. She hurried along, saying, "They'll be going to bed soon as the news is over." The sound of the radio was muted and she wondered if they were already too late.

Again, the grass rattled. Leaning into the wind, the grass brushed against her left arm. It stung. Angling a little right, away from whatever prickly stuff might be hidden amid the grass, she kept moving—until the rattling moved ahead of her, rippled back and forth across her path. She stopped, felt Margie shiver, and moved slowly forward. The grass blew back against her, stung her bare arms and legs. As Margie whimpered, she backed up. There must be some kind of weed, maybe nettles, in the grass that she couldn't see. But why hadn't they run into nettles this afternoon?

Lifting her head, she still couldn't see the house, just the bushes, almost trees, running along where the fence should be. Well, if she couldn't see forward, she'd just have to measure her progress from the summer kitchen. A quick glance over her shoulder to get a bearing on the Potter house and the garage and kitchen would soon have them back on their own path. Except she couldn't see the Potter house!

Turning completely around, she realized how tall the grass seemed now, nearly shoulder height. She couldn't see the old garage where they'd found the ladder. But that was just a short building. Without lights on, you might not see it anyway. But where was the house? With the moon shining full, the solid old three-story house should be blocking a quarter of the sky! Where was it?

Breathing through her mouth, she turned around again. And again.

She was patting Margie's shaking shoulders even before she consciously heard her sister's soft sobs.

This was stupid! You couldn't lose a house!

Another full turn.

Was the grass growing? How could it be so high? She'd been able to see all the way across the lawn to the Potter place all afternoon. She'd even been afraid someone out on the street could see in, see them in the summer kitchen.

Wait, the summer kitchen had been just steps behind them when they got turned around. She'd veered to the side to avoid the weeds, but they hadn't gone *that* far! So, where was it? Standing on tiptoe, she thought she saw something, a low roof, not that far away. Smiling, she reached down to take Margie's hand again. "This way." If the summer kitchen was *there,* their house had to be *that* way! Somehow, she'd stumbled into a patch of grass and tall weeds. But who wouldn't, wandering about in the dark? It would be all right now.

Four steps later, the grass reached out and slapped her.

Dorrie froze. Margie screamed and Dorrie didn't even attempt to shush her. Right now, being grounded, even for a whole week, would be better than this. Without shifting her feet, she reached out to push the grass aside.

It writhed under her fingers, slipped past her wrist, twined itself around her arm, covered her face. And everywhere it touched, it burned!

She threw herself backward, fell over Margie, carrying them both to the ground.

Margie's scream was so high she couldn't even hear it as the grass closed over their heads, cutting out all light, all air.

She couldn't get Margie to move, couldn't get back to her own feet. Tangling her fingers in the light cotton of her sister's dress, she crawled under the grassy canopy, pulled Margie behind her, crawled and pulled back toward the dark smudge she'd thought was the summer kitchen's roof.

If she could just get back there, she could find her way.

She found the kitchen by crawling headfirst toward it. The grass had fallen away from them yards ago, but Margie refused to get up, to walk, so Dorrie just kept pulling her.

"We're back, Margie, see?" She slapped the dark wall.

The girl's eyes, all pupils in the dim light, followed the sound and focused. Then she started screaming again. "No! No, no, no!"

"No, it's okay. We can figure out where we went wrong now, see?" Urging Margie along with her, she fumbled her way to the front door. "Look, the street is straight out from here. We can't get tangled up this time."

Twenty minutes later, they were back by the door, their faces blotchy from tears, their arms and legs stinging from the grass's latest assault. Margie had stopped screaming when they turned back toward the kitchen, and she hadn't made a sound since. Grass stems and seeds were caught in her red curls. Her lips were nearly invisible, as white as the skin beneath her freckles. She shivered continuously. Around them, the grass flowed like waves, but there was no wind.

"Let's go inside," Dorrie urged. "You're cold. Someone will find us soon. Mom and Dad will see we're not in bed."

Margie shook her head, twined her fingers around the edge of the low stone step where they huddled and stared at the grass.

"Come on."

Slowly, without taking her eyes off the grass, Margie pressed her back harder against the door.

Sliding down beside her, Dorrie searched the sky for some sign of light. It wasn't really cold. They could just stay here until morning. Someone would find them when it got light.

Hazelwood, August 11, 1998

Cashelle settled her grocery bags next to Angela's and rubbed the deep ridges the plastic handles had pressed into her fingers. "Wish they'd put a bus stop up here somewhere instead of way down at the bottom of the street."

Angela set her hands in the small of her spine and arched her back until something snapped. "Yeah, you and me both." Glancing off to the right, she pointed to the moving van in front of the Mercers' place. "There they go."

"Maybe now we'll get that bus stop."

"Whatcha mean?"

Rolling the handles of her bags into one twist, she picked them up again and shuffled forward. "Well, with them gone, they'll probably put up that apartment building now. They was the last ones to move out. You can bet the town'll have a stop in front of an apartment building, they always do."

The sun against Angela's dark hair was making her vaguely stomach sick so she was grateful for the sparse shade the heavy trees fronting the old Potter place provided. She should have worn a hat. "How come they didn't move before? I heard something about them builders offering a good dollar for the place."

"God, this street is steep!" The one twisted handle cut harder than the bunch of little ones so Cashelle stopped again in the shade to unroll them. Before picking them up again, she glanced back toward the only house on the street showing any sign of occupation. "Sort of a sad thing, really. I don't know how much of it is true, my mother heard about it. Seems they had two daughters that went missing. No one knows exactly what happened. I think Dad thought Mr. Mercer had something to do with it, but Mom always said that was just Dad's diseased brain." Cashelle laughed. "Anyway, they disappeared one day and Mrs. Mercer wouldn't move, she always thought that if they could come back, they'd come back to their own house. She was afraid to move in case they came back someday and she'd not be there." She picked up the bags and settled her arms so her elbows pressed into her waist to help support the weight while her forearms held the bags out far enough not to bang into her legs. "'Course, they never did come back."

Angela hefted her bags and followed along, looking back at the moving van. "So why they moving now?"

"Mrs. Mercer died last spring. I guess Mister decided he'd lived there long enough."

"And no one ever saw 'em?"

"Well, Mom said she saw them that day, before they went missing, out playing by the Potters' summer kitchen."

"*Summer* kitchen? What, they didn't use the same kitchen all year?"

An attempt to point and still hang on to the groceries earned Cashelle a bashed knee. "I got to get a car!" Dropping the bags and pushing her hair back out of her eyes, she pointed. "See that saggy building over there?"

"Yeah, off by itself."

"That one. Back when the place was built, they put a second kitchen out back there. It was mostly screens and big windows, cooler than cooking in the big house." She chuckled. "And less chance of burning the whole house down if you had a kitchen fire. Anyway, Mom said she saw them playing there the afternoon before they went missing."

Angela stood on tiptoe to catch a better look at the place. "Must've been shorter bushes back then. You can't hardly see anything now." A quick glance up and down the street confirmed that, other than the movers, there was no one else in sight. "Look, leave this stuff here for a minute and come with me? Have a look?"

"I don't know, Angie, I gotta get home, get supper going."

"Like anyone's going to start it without you? Not bloody likely. Come on. No one's going to steal the groceries." She grinned. "And it looks so nice and cool in there, doesn't it?"

It did. The trees' shadows danced across the wild grass. After a second, Cashelle shrugged. "Why not? Might be the last time we get to poke around the old place before the wrecking crews turn up. Mom used to say the Potters had the best garden on the street. All kinds of stuff growing in there. Maybe we can 'rescue' a few things before they dig it all up."

The breeze through the garden cooled their hot faces and Angela paused to tie her hair back to let it get at her neck as well. Cashelle was right, there were flower bed outlines everywhere. Some tiny blue flowers next to the summer kitchen's front door caught her eye. They'd sure look better in her yard than buried under an apartment building. Bending over to finger them, she found that even the leaves smelled sweet. When she stood up, Cashelle was pointing through the dirty windows.

"Looks like one of the Potters must have had an herb garden here somewhere. See all the stuff hanging from those rafters? Been there for years I'd bet."

Angela pressed her face close to the glass, shading it with one hand against the reflection of her own face. "Hey, Cashelle, looky here! See them?"

"What?" She stepped in close and peered upward. "Oh, yeah. Dried flowers." Frowning, she squinted. "What's that?" Her finger left a mark on the window when she tried to point to something specific in the dark rafters above. She rubbed it away and squinted harder. "It looks like faces. . . . Oh! Look, Angela, there's another one."

The two women turned to one another at the same moment, wide grins on their faces. With one voice, they confirmed each other's sighting: "Dolls!"

Glancing around and still seeing no one on the street, Angela dropped her voice. "Think we can sneak in there?"

Cashelle shrugged. "Can't hurt to try. Not like anyone lives here anymore. And it's all going to get torn down anyway."

Laughing like children, they hurried off to circle the building. "Must be some way in," Angela called back as she headed around back. "Meet you on the other side."

Willmington, August 14, 1998

THE WILLMINGTON STANDARD

—Still no sign of two young Hazelwood women who disappeared in that community three days ago. Although several people saw them shopping that day and their grocery bags were found on the street, no one recalls seeing the women. . . .

The Withe-Wife

B oth "The Doll House" and "The Carlisle Witch" are stories in traditional long narrative form. Either tale easily fits the length and
scope of a novella, and though it might be possible to draw some information about magical practice from these stories, magical instruction is
not the first purpose of either piece. To paraphrase the Bard, "The *story*
is the thing."

Most witch tales, like ghost stories, are meant to entertain us, to give
us a little shiver, not to provide us with a lesson in esoteric practice. In
fact, in the case of "The Doll House," it wouldn't be unreasonable to
suggest that the tale is a warning *against* indiscriminate magic. The next
piece, "The Withe-Wife," takes the witch tale in a different direction in
both form and function.

To begin with, it isn't prose at all but poetry, translated from the Welsh,
which likely began life as a song or a chant. Folklorists would class it as a
teaching ballad. Just as colonial-era fishermen had songs that described long
stretches of coastline, the depth of bays, the presence or absence of shoals,
the distance from headland to headland, and used these songs in place of
maps, other, largely illiterate groups, like women, frequently turned information into ditties that were more easily memorized than standard lists and
instructions. So, just as a grocery list isn't a story, "The Withe-Wife" isn't in

the literary sense a narrative either, not even a narrative poem. It's a recipe, a list of ingredients with instructions for their use, cast in a form that traveled well from person to person. In this case, the recipe isn't for roast duck or lamb, but for a stickman doll to snare a husband.

If "The Withe-Wife" was a true story, it wouldn't just tell us how to draw a dream man to us but also what happened after the ritual was completed. Did the couple live happily ever after, or did the withe-wife spend the rest of her married life watching her man put one foot ahead of the other along their garden path, each time wondering if, this time, he could get away from her? At least one Welsh folktale, "The Round Road," further explores the husband's plight, portraying him much as *The Blair Witch Project*'s film students, who, regardless of logic, could find no way out from the witch's influence. However, only "The Withe-Wife," the how-to manual, seems to have made its way to American shores.

The Withe-Wife

Fingers dance in the sweet spring grass.
Timothy for constancy,
Myrtle for grace,
Lavender for bed-love sated through Winter Pass.

Threads of a dream, spin now in the sun.
Marsh-maid to draw,
Heather to keep,
Withe to seal his path beside her.

Twisting together, strands knotted at Full.

Hands without fingers,

Legs without feet,

A face without features, soon to meet.

Through the Dark Face, it lurks.

Water upon it,

Sweet smoke below,

A prickling to bind it, touched by the crow.

Figure of hope cast out on a new tide.

A far man finds it,

In finding, keeps,

To abandon his own, a withe-wife to seek.

Her roads rise to meet him, no failing this dawn.

Green turns gold,

Autumn comes red,

Pale face shudders, lost in her bed.

This, the earliest known translation into English of "The Withe-Wife" isn't the most graceful ever done. The quickest scan reveals that little effort was made to adapt it to a comfortable rhythm or rhyme scheme. As the purpose of the original Welsh song was to make the ritual easier to remember, this lack of poetic attention in America may seem odd, even

counterproductive. For a narrative poem, yes. Clumsy meter and rhyme schemes aside, however, this version of "The Withe-Wife" is a near word-for-word translation. The obvious conclusion, then, is that the content was the important factor. Later versions would prove more harmonious to the English-language ear, but this first one remains the most accurate, and it's from this version that the ritual itself can be re-created.

First of all, we learn that the summoning and binding ritual wasn't an impulsive act. The time frame begins in the early spring, with set activities at particular times, and doesn't end until winter is well established; the "pale face" shuddering in the Withe-Wife's bed would take some time to lose its warm-weather tan. The timing for each section of the ritual isn't expressed in dates or even days and months, but by celestial events that couldn't be mistaken. "In the sun" doesn't mean any old sunny day, but the day following the longest day of the year; "the Full" refers only to the first full moon following the longest day; "the Dark Face" the next new moon; and "the new tide" the very next turning after that new moon. In all, a very specific timetable.

The actual combination of grasses, twigs, and plants couldn't be clearer than the list given here—if you happen to know that "marsh-maid" is more commonly known as comfrey on this side of the ocean and that "withe" is a grass of coastal salt marshes. And, for all that magical rituals were supposedly wreathed in mystery, this one is laid out plainly for anyone to read or, in the case of the oral song, to hear. The fourth stanza describes how the doll must be kept from the light during the new moon,

Left: Followers of the alchemical side of magical tradition believe the totem dolls used by "granny witches" and "wise women" to be corruptions of the human-within-a-pentacle imagery common in medieval texts.

sprinkled with water, passed through "sweet" smoke, and touched with the practitioner's blood before it becomes a potent amulet. That "water" referred to dew collected during a full moon, that smoke would be sweet if it came from burning a mixture of herbs, and that blood would be drawn by stabbing the finger with the sharpened quill of a crow would all have been understood by those passing and receiving the song.

Still, even though the poem is clearly a formula for magical ritual and not a traditional story, it, like "The Doll House" and *The Blair Witch Project,* hints at the misery caused by using poppets or stickmen or withemen to pull the victim from his or her life's path. The last line of "The Withe-Wife" doesn't, as some might infer, leave us with the image of a man lost in the throes of passion. In the Welsh, the man's "shudder" is one of terror, not ecstasy, and he is, literally, "lost" in his wife's bed, unable to escape. He's her prisoner, not her partner.

"The Corn Man," the last of this sampling of stickman tales, is like "The Withe-Wife" a translation. Unlike "The Withe-Wife," it became a song after enjoying a considerable time as a straightforward narrative. Collected into New England's oral story collections around 1780, it has always been attributed to "a local Indian tribe," but, clearly less politically sensitive than current mores demand, the storytellers failed to pass along such relevant details as who made the translation or even which tribal tradition had created the original.

Still, while the song's provenance fails to meet the most basic guidelines for literary scholarship or study, the relevance of its content to fans of *The Blair Witch Project* certainly earns it a place in this particular collection of witch tales.

The Corn Man

Twisting, twisting,
twisting in trees,
Dancing, dancing,
tho there's no breeze.

Corn man, corn man, point me the way,
Turn, now, before night steals day.
Corn man, corn man, show me the way!

Please, please,
let a foundered soul flee.
Forgive these hands,
that ever fouled thee.

Corn doll, corn doll, show me the way,
Night threatens to hold me, bind me, slay.
Corn man, corn man, show me the way!

Darkness has settled,
all over this hill,
Yet, in silence,
the corn dolls dance still.

Corn man, corn man, is your lady here?

Does she step softly, closer to hear?

Corn man, corn man, is your lady so near?

Leaving you, finding you,

at the same turn.

Dying or smiling,

lessons last learned.

Corn man, corn man, I know the way.

Step and step, one course to stay.

Corn man, corn man, I've found the way.

Whether as stories, songs, poems, or films, the essential story, the rule for encounters between people and "poppets," remains the same: Don't touch! In every such tale, regardless of medium or source, the penalty for handling a witch's stickman is imprisonment in some strange back eddy of reality where north is south, out is in, and mere mortals, even those with maps and compasses, can't hope to escape.

the stones

When reviewers and critics describe *The Blair Witch Project* as unique, they're usually referring to its production and promotion. Other than Orson Welles's "War of the Worlds," what other media project ever managed to so thoroughly convince its audience of its own reality? What other film ever made it into general release without a *script*? And, in what other film were the actors also the film crew?

Without doubt, *The Blair Witch Project* greatly expanded the concept of "audience experience" with its Internet promotion and the release of the TV special *Curse of the Blair Witch*. *The Blair Witch Project* is probably the first, and only, film *designed* to be experienced in multiple entertainment media, with each experience building on the others to greatly enhance the film's aura of reality. No longer will films stay safely inside the theater!

While *The Blair Witch Project* was busy redefining the technical aspects of film production, the film was also drawing heavily on the well-established icons and imagery of New World, specifically American New World, occult folklore for its storyline. What seems remarkable on its face is that, despite the inclusion of numerous significant occult icons within the Blair Witch myth, both Myrick and Sánchez claim to have less than a passing acquaintance with that nearly four-hundred-year-old supernatural history.

Folklorists like Toronto's Moira Paige aren't surprised by that. "Everyone on the planet has probably heard a ghost story at some time. When we were kids, the big thing was 'Mirror Mary,' a story about a woman who lived in the mirror. You could call her out of it by lighting a candle in front of a mirror, turning off the rest of the lights, and saying 'Mirror Mary' three times. There were all sorts of stories explaining how she got into the mirror in the first place—most pretty gory—but regardless of why she was in there, everyone knew that the first thing she'd do when she got out was tear someone's face off! Still, when we got older, we sort of forgot about that story—until the film *Candyman* scared us all over again.

"The point is, we often forget the specifics of any legend until we're put in a situation where remembering has some context. Say 'witch' and 'rock' in the same sentence, ask someone to remember a story about witches and rocks, and you'll probably draw a blank look. Start to tell them one story about witches, though, and they'll probably recall a completely different story, one they haven't thought about in years, and nine times out of ten, *that* story will have something to do with the rocks you were prompting them to remember in the first place. Memory is often an associative function rather than a direct one."

And how does this help account for the commonality of images, such as the piles of stones found outside the fictional filmmakers' tent or the rocks found twined in the tree branches? How might those particular images, present in a considerable number of early witch tales, find themselves in Sánchez and Myrick's film if they'd never heard those stories, even as children?

Moira Paige, like everyone else who's remarked on the similarity of certain portions of *The Blair Witch Project* to existing legends, has a theory: "Aside from the obvious possibility that their creative minds were unconsciously drawing on stories they'd heard previously, there's also a certain cultural bias, a group symbolism, that might suggest particular items as appropriate props. Despite being as common as, well, dirt, stones do have a symbolic value in Western culture. Menhirs, the huge stones that

Right: From these massive menhirs to New Age crystal therapy, there is an unbroken tradition of linking stones to mysticism.

form circles as found at Stonehenge in England and the Rich Ring in Arkansas, have long associations with magical rites. The stones of early burial cairns often remained untouched, even when other rocks are gathered in the same area, because of their connection to death, which is, in many cultures including our own, a highly ritualized, near-magical event. In Great Britain, the English and the Scots are still arguing about a rock that raises nationalistic hackles in both countries, a rock that supposedly has magical properties. In Ireland, there's the Blarney Stone. Descendants of these parts of Europe are probably primed to accept stones as appropriate items for magical uses.

"Then there's mainstream associations. As symbols of barrenness, death, or loss, stones have a prominent place in literature, especially poetry. Bread and hearths, spring, fire, and candles mean life, home, and safety; frogs, winter, ice, the moon, and piles of stones arouse thoughts of mysticism and death."

Predating *The Blair Witch Project* by about two hundred years and just over one hundred years respectively, "Children of Stone" and "The Stone Sorcerer" are both prime examples of the continuity of such occult symbolism.

Children of Stone

The woman's heels drummed the damp soil as they dragged her up Thorn Hill. Her tangled mat of dark hair hid most of her face. The gag shoved in her mouth protected them from the worst of her profanities and blasphemies. Yet, more than one woman gathered around the hanging platform thought it had been a mistake to outfit the witch in sackcloth. Though it was meant to demean and debase the body, on this woman it managed to entice the glances of Drumheller's most confirmed bachelors, its staunchest churchmen, even its oldest grandfathers. Something in the way she strained against the ropes that held her arms behind her back, the frantic arching of her back, could make even the witchfinder's eyes follow her shambling progress between her jailors.

"She doesn't seem so happy to be meeting her dark lover this time!" A voice, attributable to no particular man, called from the rear of the crowd.

As she reached the two low steps, the witch's struggles grew frenzied. The half-rotten cloth that barely covered her threatened to split when the men to either side hauled her off her feet and up over those steps. "I wager she'd prefer a man's member now!" another voice bellowed back. Scattered laughter greeted that comment but was quickly hushed by the glares of decent women come to see justice carried out.

Those nearest the temporary staging, considerably less jolly than those to the rear, flinched visibly when the witch's undulating wail began, but the sound didn't prevent them from tossing the sturdy rope over the timbers erected above the platform, and it didn't drown out the reading of charge, verdict, and sentence. The wail rose to a stifled scream when the noose settled on her shoulders and they began cutting away long hanks of the snarled hair.

For the first time, the crowd could truly see the witch's face. The threatening skies provided even, shadowless illumination, stark and revealing. Despite the screams and struggles, no color rose in her cheeks. Against that pallor, every bruise and mark, from the purple ring of the pillory around her neck to the star-shaped burn high on one cheek, stood out clearly. The hollow at the base of her throat, fluttering madly as she struggled to draw breath around the gag in her mouth, held the last evidence against her, the small dark circle that Early Marlbone, the witch-finder from England, had immediately recognized for the devil's teat.

Marlbone wasn't presenting evidence today. Instead of the passionate witness, he was an almost colorless minor figure on the platform, merely holding the basket into which the witch's hair was being gathered. It would be buried with the rest of her less than a hundred feet away. The hole was already open down on the beach. Two men leaned against their shovels as they waited to perform their part and fill in the base grave before the encroaching tide covered it. Marlbone had been very specific on how a witch's remains should be handled. The salt water leaching over her corpse twice daily, he'd assured them, would ensure Drumheller's safety from satanic forces.

The meetings to determine when and how the witch be executed had been well attended, with interested observers coming from as far as sixty miles away. The event itself was drawing hundreds. The Drumheller Council had even, at one point, considered roping off the hill and charging an admission. Only rumbling discontent at the idea of "blood money" had finally dissuaded them. From the looks on some of those councillors' faces as scores more arrived just as the last lock of hair fell into the basket, they might well be regretting the lost opportunity for revenues. Wagons hauled off along Thorn Hill Way held yet more visitors, figuring to get a better view from their higher seats.

Of all those gathered around the hill, only one family seemed anxious to leave.

Karl Tanner eased his team back slowly, wary of the tight confines that might spook even the best horses. Mary's hand on his arm silently urged him on, but it wasn't necessary. He was as anxious as she to escape. Memories of himself as a small boy in Lehr, of mobs roaming the street night after night, bursting into homes in search of icons or beads, easily merged with the events unfolding around him.

As the team pulled left and away from the line of wagons, Mary slid closer to his side. He couldn't make out the soft words she murmured while he searched for a piece of drier ground on which to turn the team around. He didn't need to. Whatever prayers Mary was composing, whether for their escape from this crowd that could so easily become a mob, or for the rain to hold off long enough for them to reach some other town tonight, or even for the safe repose of the soul inside that poor creature up there, they would all find favor with him.

He was almost to the water's edge before he found a trackless area that looked less likely to bog his wheels than the churned ground behind him. Mary leaned into the turn with him, clucking softly to the horses. The road back was rising before them when the entire crowd seemed to take a step up the hill as one. "Hurry, Karl," Mary said.

A gentle flick of the reins wrapped back and forth between his fingers brought the team one gait up from a walk. One by one, they passed the other wagons. Mary's hand rested on his shoulder as she turned to look back at the hilltop. A collective hush gripped the crowd, allowing what was said above to drift even as far as the road.

The witch-finder was insisting that even a witch be given the chance to confess her sins. Therefore, even though she'd denied the charges against her before—despite the overwhelming evidence to the contrary—the most senior churchman in Drumheller stood forth on the platform to play out his role once again. This time, however, he stood far enough away that she could neither kick nor spit at him. His voice carried easily out over the crowd, entreating her to divest herself through public contrition. "For there is no remedy, no further recourse, for the dead. . . ."

Whatever her response was, it was lost due to the gag in her mouth. The pastor, reddening in response to the scattered sniggers passing through the audience, motioned for someone to remove the dirty ball of cloth. "Do you intend to speak, then?"

For a moment, she said nothing, merely passed her tongue over her lips as she stared down at the hole on the beach. From the height of the hill, it was obvious that water was already seeping up through the bottom of it. Her eyes closed briefly. Karl and Mary Tanner couldn't hear her first few words. Even Marlbone had to strain to catch them: "Not even a stone to mark me."

The churchman frowned. "There is no hope of mortal redemption for you here, only the chance to refute your master and hope for unearthly mercy."

She nodded and lifted her head to speak clearly, loudly. "I have spent my life as a God-fearing woman." Grumbling protests began at once. She continued more loudly. "I have loved my God—and still do. But, for you, you who would try me without reason, who would love me so little as to speak lies about me for your own gain, who would begrudge me so much as a smooth stone that would cost you naught, I have no love, nor forgiveness, in my heart!"

"It is not we who ask *your* forgiveness, witch!" The pastor's hand rose as if to smack her down but Early Marlbone caught it. "You?" He stared down at the small witch-finder, "*You* would condone this speech?"

Marlbone shrugged easily. "No, but, in my experience, there are many who, at the end, would trade their co-conspirators for the chance of heavenly rewards. Let her speak, good sir, and perhaps she will reveal that which she has kept hidden these months."

Throughout the brief exchange, the woman had ignored the men

beside her to let her gaze linger on first one, then another, of the faces staring up at her. Several stared back at her, but more flinched away. When a movement at the back of the crowd caught her eye, she let her attention follow the wagon slowly moving back along Thorn Hill Way. When next she spoke, her voice had softened. It carried as far as before, but the anger seemed to bleed away with each word:

> *Twelve and one nests will bear stones for me,*
> *Twelve and one coupled beasts will bear stones for me.*
> *And, for each of the twelve and one of you who would grant me such*
> * rest,*
> *Twelve and one barren wombs will bear stones for me.*
> *Let your women suckle those babes at their breast!*
> *Or let me rest.*

Out in the wagon, Mary gasped and her hand fell to the shallow curve of her belly just beginning to strain against her skirts. For the briefest moment, her eyes met those of the woman on the hill.

The witch's lips curved into a sad smile as three men burst from the crowd. Others followed. In seconds, the crowd surged over the platform as the pale face with its wan smile disappeared from view.

"Oh, Father above, Karl, what has she done?"

Heedless of those beside them, Karl slapped the reins, brought the horses up to a trot before they had even made it back to the main road.

His arm held her close to his side. "What has she done? Left this accursed town in her own way."

"But what she said . . ." Mary shook her head.

The horses found their footing as the wagon rattled up to the roadway. Wind whipped past them and, breathless, Mary turned her face into her husband's shoulder and closed her eyes.

They would drive the horses for a solid day before coming upon New Harbor and, still, the image of the woman's eyes resting on her hung before Mary's eyes.

Early Marlbone watched the water inch its way up the shoreline. Each wave traveled a little farther over the new grave, smoothing it, hiding it from view. It had taken some time to gather up the pieces that were all the crowd left behind. Water had been lapping at the edge of the grave before his shouted warnings had brought some order to the scene. The Pastor and councillors, as enraged as their neighbors, had proved useless and in the end it had been Marlbone himself who took control of the jailors and the gravediggers, who waded into the crowd to reclaim the witch's remains and put all the pieces safely below ground.

Now he shook his head as he watched over the grave. So scared they were of the woman's curse, yet they'd been prepared to ignore the clearer threat posed by the presence of her mortal self scattered across their commons. Even now he doubted that they'd understood anything he'd told them. The fools! So, he sat, watching, waiting, ensuring no angry townsman thought to continue his attack on the witch's body and, in the process, endanger them all.

Young David was nowhere to be seen when Millicent appeared in the kitchen to start breakfast for the household, but the basket of eggs sat on the table and the wood box was well stocked, so she wasn't as displeased as she might have been. If he was back with the family's ration of butter and milk in the next few minutes, she wouldn't mention his tardiness to Pastor Thomas this time. Instead, she stuck her head out the door and waved to attract the attention of the two housemaids, who'd begun boiling water in the backyard for the day's wash.

"If you see that boy before I do, hurry him along. The Pastor doesn't like to wait on his breakfast this time of the year."

As it happened, she'd just stoked the fire and hung her cloak nearby when the boy burst into the kitchen. "Whoa there, boy!" She flicked his ear sharply. "I hope you've not run all the way like that? You'll separate the milk!"

The boy laughed and shook his head. "No, ma'am, I walked it just like you said. I just hurried a bit when Mabel threatened to wallop me with that paddle!" With a great deal more care than he'd shown for the milk, he laid the small pail of butter on the counter.

Millicent laughed. The paddles the girls used to stir the laundry were a serious threat and Mabel was a sturdy young woman with a lot of strength in her arms from tackling the heavy wet sheets. "Well, next time, you'd best get things done on time."

"I would've, if'n not for that dead bird."

"Dead bird?"

"One of the new lot of hens. Was dead there this morning and I had to take it down to Mr. Hant before the others pecked it apart."

The oats had soaked overnight and needed nothing more than to be moved over the heat and stirred until they plumped properly, so, after handing David a spoon and seeing him settled on the stool, Millicent turned to the rest of the meal. While she heated and buttered the largest pan, she listened with half an ear to David's description of Albert Hant's disgust at losing a brand-new bird. "Fair went purple, he did!" The boy held his breath but couldn't quite achieve the right effect. "Last I saw him, he was stomping off to tell the Pastor. Said he was thinking to go and demand a replacement."

Millicent was about to comment on the unlikely event that anyone would get a replacement hen out of a Drumheller farmer as she snicked the first of the morning's eggs smartly against the side of her bowl, but the dull *thunk* and chip of pottery that skittered across the table drove all thoughts of disgruntled hen-men out of her mind. Blinking, she ran a finger over the bowl's broken rim. A tracery of cracks radiated from the chipped lip. It was ruined. It took some seconds more for her to notice the egg, round and perfect, still cradled in her hand.

David stirred as she rolled the egg in her hand, hefted it, then ran a finger over the smooth surface. "Didn't break it?"

She rounded on him before he realized his perilous position, grabbing his shirtfront, smacking him back against the oven's brickwork. "Think it's funny, do you? A fun bit of mischief, eh?" Spit sprayed him when her reddened face pressed close. "That bowl cost money, boy, and I'm not going to be out its cost for your prank!" Heedless of the oats just beginning to bubble, she dragged him down off the high stool and hauled him behind her as she headed for the stairway, pausing only to shake the egg under his nose whenever the mood struck her.

"Wait! I didn't do it! I was only stirring the pot!"

"How long did you have it, eh? How long did you think about it?" She shook him again, then dragged him through the doorway and up the stairs. "Well, you'll have lots of time to think about it now!"

The Pastor, still stiff from the buffeting he'd taken atop Thorn Hill when the crowd surged over the platform, was in no mood for trouble from "below stairs." The only thing he wanted to see Millicent hauling up here was breakfast, not some squalling kitchen wretch. His silent appeal to his wife, who sat mending at the far end of the table, gained him nothing. She had no love for the irritable cook. The tangled tale Millicent spun him, of eggs, burnt oats, and dead capons, made no more sense the fourth time around than the first! David's increasingly loud denials of wrongdoing couldn't make it any more intelligible. The Pastor, however, prided himself on being able to cut to the heart of any issue. Turning to his cook, he delivered the decisive question. "And, how could an *egg* have broken a bowl?"

"Because it's not an egg!" Transferring her grip to her assistant's ear, the cook stomped to the end of the dining room table and dropped the egg next to the English china. It thumped and rolled, whole, into his lap. She grinned as he juggled it, watching him realize, as she had, that anything capable of withstanding the original fall wasn't vulnerable to a soft lap. "It's a stone! Thought it would be a lovely trick, he did."

"I didn't!"

"Don't compound your sin with lies, boy."

"But, I'm not lying, sir. I just collected the eggs, same as always."

"Mark?" Eunice was standing at his elbow. He hadn't seen her move. "May I see the egg?"

"It's *not* an egg!" Millicent protested. "It's a rock."

Eunice stroked the egg-shaped object gently, "Yes, I see that." She smiled as she picked it from her husband's palm. "Well, you might as well go on back to the kitchen, Millicent. The Pastor and I will handle it from here."

"But . . ."

"That will be all, Millicent. It was just a bowl after all."

When the cook had stamped back down the stairs, Eunice closed the stairwell door before turning to the boy. "So, David, you collected the eggs this morning?"

"Yes, ma'am, like always. I didn't put nothing else in the basket except the eggs." He crossed himself quickly and added, "God's truth."

"Hmm. I see." She nodded once. "Yes, I think I *do* see, now. I think you should go back to your chores now, David."

"You believe me?"

"Yes."

The boy stood there for another few seconds, then sprinted for the door.

"Oh, David?"

His sigh as he drew up just short of the door was audible to both adults. "Yes, ma'am?"

"Have Mr. Hant come see me about that hen, would you?"

"Ah, yes, ma'am."

Eunice smiled as the little boy slipped out the door and clattered down the stairs but turned serious when she laid the stone egg back on the table. "I hope your Mr. Marlbone hasn't left us yet."

Early Marlbone studied the latest stone to be delivered into his keeping. It was becoming something of a ritual. Friday morning would dawn, he'd eat his breakfast, and, sometime between then and suppertime, the Pastor would arrive with another stone. Another stone and a question. "How can this be happening? We did everything you said."

Marlbone's assurances that no witch could survive submersion in salt water weren't enough. Rumors of the "witch's curse" sped from house to house with each new stone's discovery. The obvious answer—that someone, some living sympathizer was at work, making it *appear* that the witch could reach beyond her grave—couldn't gain a foothold against such rampant superstition. He swore softly. One man couldn't keep watch on every chicken coop in Drumheller.

He consoled himself with the thought that this couldn't continue forever. Planting a few beach rocks in the nests of naive farmers was easy enough. The next part of the curse would prove impossible for even the most determined human being to contrive.

Marlbone tapped the rocks one by one. Ten more to come. If the residents of Drumheller could be prevented from indulging another outburst like the one on Thorn Hill, this would all be over in just ten weeks.

A dairyman for sixty-two of his seventy-six years, Calvin Drover had never seen an animal struggle as this one did to drop its calf. Deep shudders wracked the floundering animal that thrashed on the blood-soaked hay. Three men crouched over her. Alice, his youngest daughter-in-law, a woman stouthearted enough to have washed her man's entrails and sew them back inside him when he'd been gored by a horn in midwinter, had fled when the cow's panting turned to anguished moans and high-pitched squeals.

Calvin gripped the edge of the stall hard when he saw the next pain overtake the poor animal. Buttercup, they'd called this one. Not for the flowers she loved to wrap her long tongue around, but for the thick layer of cream that came from every bucket of her milk. As her eyes rolled back in her head and spasms jerked her legs against the ropes that tied her in place, Calvin doubted she'd last another hour. Blood gushed from her heaving body as the contraction took full control.

"Mother of God!" Malcolm, elbow-deep in the cow, searching vainly for some grip on the calf that might help bring it forth, gasped as the muscles clamped down on his forearm.

"Enough!" Calvin shook his head at the men in the stall. "Jamie, lad, run and get the mattock. Malcolm, get yourself out of there. It's no use." He waved off their denials. "I'll not have her suffer anymore. Go, Jamie."

At a nod from his father, Calvin's great-grandson picked himself out of the hay and fled to the shed for the heavy hammer. Aaron, sitting back on his heels, laid a hand on Malcolm's shoulder. "He's right, man. There's nothing else you can do."

Still sprawled on the floor, Malcolm shook his head, rode out the contraction, and pressed his hand forward again. "I've brought out difficult calves before."

"Not like this one, man. It's hours you've been at it, you know, and not so much as a nose or a foot have you found. It's no good."

The arm Malcolm dragged back was blue from the pressure of the great bones and muscles grinding against it. He rubbed it idly as they waited for the boy to come back. "I don't understand it."

Another contraction seized the cow as they watched. The low rattle at the end of her weak bleating told them it was only a matter of time before the powerful heart would stop itself. Aaron reached for the heavy knife he'd taken from Alice's neat kitchen. "Perhaps we can at least salvage the calf."

When Jamie rushed back with the hammer, Malcolm took it and ordered him back outside. "Go ask your mother to boil us some water for the washing up."

The dairyman's blow was true. Between one breath and the next, the cow's struggles ceased and, with a single deep stroke, Aaron laid open the Jersey's ruddy side. The swollen uterus bulged through the cut, but there was no telltale flicker of movement inside it. Calvin was shaking his head again when Aaron leaned forward for the second cut. "I knew that cow felt wrong. And now we've lost both in trying too long to save the cow."

All three men paused when Aaron's practiced stroke rasped across something hard. "What the . . . ?" More slowly, he enlarged the slit. The smooth white stone that slid from the now-flaccid muscle defied their combined one hundred and thirty-one years of experience.

Hobbling around the end of the stall, Calvin nudged the bloodied object with his stick.

It rolled toward Malcolm's feet.

Aaron backed away from the butchered animal. "It's not possible. Not possible."

The three blood-splattered men were still staring when Alice, with Aaron's new bride, Detta, and Jamie on her heels, flew in through the byre's Dutch door. As often happened in the Drover house, it was Alice who put words to the men's thoughts. "Coupled beasts will bear stones for me. . . ." But not even Alice would repeat the rest, not with Detta, rosy and plump with her fourth child, gripping the head of the stall.

Marlbone crouched on the damp sand to inspect the latest pile of stones. They'd stopped bringing them to him. Now, to appease the spirit of a dead witch, the people of Drumheller brought them to the beach and piled them in untidy cairns. Marlbone knew the stones could not have all been taken from dead cattle and pigs. He'd hauled away dozens already. A new pile sprang up daily. Confronting the fearful men and women who brought them accomplished nothing. They'd lost faith in him. He, the man who'd first identified the witch in their midst!

Taking up the top stone of this new pile, he flung it out over the bay, watched it sink.

Stupid fools!

They hadn't even put the stones over the body!

Whatever remained of the shattered woman lay at least fifty feet farther east.

Deliberately throwing each stone along a different trajectory, he cleared the pile once more. Only two of them showed the telltale bloodstains. Surely it was almost over.

When he turned to walk back Thorn Hill Way, he saw the woman standing on the hill again, watching him. He was no primitive soul to be startled into thinking he'd encountered the witch's shade come back to accuse him. He'd recognize Eunice's upright posture, her light footsteps, and untutored grace even in the dark. They nodded silently to each other, then turned for the walk back to town.

Pastor Mark Hayward groped for his wife's hand under the blanket that covered them in the second seat of Early Marlbone's wagon. Marlbone, seated on the first seat with Amelia Gray perched next to him giving directions, drove like a madman.

Eunice's hand squeezed her husband's gently and, in a voice pitched low enough not to carry forward, murmured, "It's not far now."

The Pastor had been called out for a laboring woman only a half-dozen times in the past ten years. More often, the knock in the middle of the night was to summon Eunice. Though they'd not been blessed with children of their own, Eunice had gained a reputation for being able to coax recalcitrant babes forth, for turning a child laying wrong in the womb, and for easing pain with distilled essences she made from the plants in her garden. So the Pastor had been startled when young Amelia had said her mother was asking for both of them. He hoped it was nothing more than the latest manifestation of the growing fear in Drumheller. He doubted that Early's arrival at the parsonage, in a wagon with seats enough for the four of them, was as fortunately coincidental as the witch-finder had implied.

They heard the woman's screams even before Early brought the team to a full halt.

Inside the small house, Eunice spoke briefly with one of the women in the kitchen. She handed a small bottle to a second woman with instructions to add several spoonfuls to a cup of warm tea and bring it to the bedroom right away. She didn't stop Early Marlbone from following her, but suggested to her husband that he speak with Mr. Gray while she checked on Mrs. Gray. When she eased the door closed behind her, Marlbone had already retreated to a far corner, out of her way, but still able to keep the sweat-soaked woman under his watchful eye.

Emma Gray's legs trembled as Eunice slid the hem of her nightdress high.

"Your first child since Amelia, isn't it?" The woman couldn't speak, just nodded as she reached for the sheet tied between the bedposts. "Happens this way sometimes, when there's a few years between babies. Let's see how this one is lying, shall we?" Even Eunice's lightest touch brought moans from Emma Gray. Fortunately, the next contraction, long and strong, took all the woman's attention. She didn't see what Early did, the first hints of fear, the numerous swift touches that clearly answered none of Eunice's silent questions.

Eunice's face was calm again by the time the contraction passed and Emma's eyes focused on her. "Have you felt much movement from this one?" Emma shook her head. "Well, let's see if we can figure out what it's been up to, shall we?" Leaning over the bed, she set her hands to either side of the distended belly. "This is going to hurt, but I won't be long, I promise."

Before Emma could protest or her body could tighten again, Eunice pressed deeply against one side, sliding her opposing hand down and then sharply upward. Emma's back arched off the bed. Her scream rang in Early's ears long after her eyes rolled back and she fell still. He stepped forward to hover beside the bed. "Is she . . . ?"

"Dead? No, Mr. Marlbone, not yet." Eunice's hands shifted again. The great curve of Emma's belly heaved. "Though it's probably just as well she can't feel this." Reaching back, she grabbed his hand and laid it on the smooth skin. "What do you feel?"

"Warmth."

"But no movement, no bumps to distinguish a foot from a head." She laid her hand atop his and moved it slowly over Emma Gray's stomach. "It's smooth isn't it?" Eunice turned to stare back at him over her shoulder. "Smooth as a stone."

Early yanked his hand from her grip and stumbled back to his spot in the corner where he shook his head, as he saw a contraction ripple across Emma's stomach. The woman groaned softly but didn't rouse. "That's impossible," he said.

"Why? Because you say so?" Eunice's hand slid down between her patient's thighs, probing deeply. "Because you throw rocks into the water?"

"The witch is dead!" Early watched as the contraction eased and fresh blood ran freely over Eunice's hand and into the mattress. "This business of stones is nothing to do with that woman. Her 'curse,' it's nothing but superstition and someone's idea of mischief!"

Eunice's eyes closed as another seizure started almost immediately. "This woman cannot pass what she's carrying inside her. I can feel it hard against my fingertips. Will you take my word that it's no child grinding itself against her bones?" The face she lifted to him when she opened her eyes was paler than her patient's. "Or must I guide your hands to it before you will believe?" When he said nothing, her bloody hand snaked forward to grab his. Early marveled at her strength, at the effort necessary to free himself from the tiny woman.

The sudden appearance of the woman who'd been left in charge of the tea allowed him to escape through the open door. He didn't pause in the front room. He didn't stop until he stood outside in the cold. He listened to the silence, to the renewed wails of the doomed young woman, to the next, longer, silence, and, finally, to the sobs of an eight-year-old child

and her father. Early Marlbone stayed there until the sun began to rise and the exhausted Haywards hauled themselves back into the wagon.

No waves could scatter the stones in the waist-high cairn that Early Marlbone had erected on a particular square of beach below Thorn Hill. Eunice could see that long before she picked her way down to the water's edge. Up close, the fading evening light was enough to let her spot a familiar egg-shaped stone among the scores that Early had lugged across the sand to this spot. It was only when she rounded the pile, however, that she saw Early Marlbone himself. Leaning back against the grave markers, the setting sun lending false color to his skin, she could almost believe that he'd merely paused to rest a bit.

Tucking her skirts around her legs, she sank down beside him and watched the sun sink farther into the bay. If she waited a little longer, until the encroaching waves lapped around the stones, she would be sure that no one else would ever see the dark blood that stained the sand beneath the witch-finder's wrists.

In a new house on the outskirts of New Harbor, Mary Tanner wriggled deeper under the quilts and pulled her daughter close to nurse once more before they both settled in for some hard-earned sleep. Out in the other room, the midwife was taking a cup of tea before Karl returned her to her own family and what remained of the night's rest.

The woman's soft voice carried clearly through the doorway. "I'd like to take credit for it, but, frankly, I'm not sure I did anything at all. . . ."

David watched as Eunice laid the first spring flowers on the lonely grave just outside the cemetery fence, then, from somewhere in his cavernous pockets, he pulled a water-smoothed stone no bigger than his palm and pushed it into the dirt.

Eunice smiled and the young boy blushed before running back along the path toward the kitchen, where Millicent would be waiting impatiently for him to stir the oats.

The Stone Sorcerer

Loudonville, New York, had precisely one claim to fame when Willa Farraugh arrived, Loudon Cottage, and she wasted no time knocking on its neat door. Somewhere in the tiny house was a closet. Inside the closet hung a single dress, white satin, elegant, bought new for Miss

Clara Harris. Of course, no one had seen the dress since it was last worn: in Box 7 of Ford's Theater on the night Abraham Lincoln was shot. As she waited for someone to answer her knock, she realized that the dress wouldn't be white anymore, or not completely so. It took little for her imagination to conjure an image of it spotted with bits of brain and the blood of a President.

Willa wasn't surprised when the door was answered by someone other than Clara Harris. Local gossip claimed that since retreating to this small town in upstate New York, Clara Harris remained cloistered inside Loudon Cottage, seeing no one but family and a few close friends. Not that anyone was all that anxious to visit these days anyway.

The tall, thin man at the door glanced up and down the street before letting his gaze settle on Willa. "Yes, what do you want?"

"I've business with Miss Clara Harris."

"Really? And you would be?"

"Willa Farraugh. I've come about the ghost."

The door slammed shut, just inches from her nose.

Sighing, she lifted her hand once more. "It won't leave on its own, you know," she whispered. Her knocks were louder than her words and, before long, the good citizens of Loudonville were slowing their steps as they promenaded down the main street. A few stopped altogether, staring at Willa's stout figure as she continued to pound on the door.

Willa could forgive them that rudeness. It was one thing to have it rumored that one of your neighbors was being haunted by the President of the U.S. of A., another thing altogether to have an elderly woman in the rune-marked cape and bone amulets of a stone witch hammering on that neighbor's door in broad daylight! She'd trade garlic bulbs for gold nuggets that no one in Loudonville had ever seen her like before. She grinned as she continued to bang away at the door. Switching hands, Willa paused only long enough to tuck a braid of gray hair, strands of bright spell-cord woven through it, back over her shoulder and cast a surreptitious glance behind her in the process. Half a dozen people were actually leaning on the wrought-iron fence that hemmed in the shallow yard, grinning, pointing, and giggling among themselves, looking away whenever her gaze might chance on theirs. Just the curious then, nothing to cause her real concern.

"Mr. Harris! I just need a moment with your daughter!"

Willa stumbled when the door was yanked open from under her hand in midknock. A young woman, in brown broadcloth and a long apron, peered around the door. There was no mistaking this plain creature with her oatmeal complexion for the diminutive beauty she'd seen in the New York newspaper. "The master says to take yourself off. No one in this house will speak with you." The girl's fingers gripped the edge of the door tightly as Willa leaned against the jamb and pulled a thin black cigar from her pocket. She sniffed it appreciatively for a second, watching the girl, who was clearly a maid of some order, occasionally peek back into the dark hallway. "Go on, now."

"I'm not going anywhere until I've seen Miss Clara Harris."

"The master won't let you in."

"Then I'll wait for her to come out." Tucking the cigar back in her pocket, Willa strolled to the edge of the street and sat next to the gate. The sun was setting, warming the dark fabric of her dress and cloak, and Willa stretched her legs out straight ahead of her. Her valise, little more than a carpetbag, made a comfortable support in the small of her back. Digging out her cigar once more, she decided this would be a fine place to enjoy it. With a wry glance at the people who still stood about watching her, she waggled it between her fingers before asking the man nearest her for a light.

She'd taken only a few warm drags when the maid slipped through the front door, bustled down the short path, and leaned close. "Master'll see you, for a moment, in the kitchen. Just go around the back way." She was pointing to a worn track in the lawn when Willa swept past her, up the walkway, and through that neat front door. She closed it sharply behind her, cutting off a startled, "Madam!"

Mr. Harris, who definitely wasn't the source of his daughter's beautiful classic features, frowned down at her. "What's this all about, then?"

"It's not you I've come to speak with."

"Clara's not up to receiving visitors, especially strangers intent on stirring up gossip." He folded his arms across his chest. "You can either say your piece to me and go on your way or you can keep it to yourself and go on your way. It's much the same to me."

"I doubt I'd be feeling too sociable myself if I'd had a ghost clambering about in my room half the night." Willa glanced around her. The house was small but well proportioned. A spotless front room extended to the left of the front door; to the right, an elegant rail followed a dog-leg stairway to the upper floor. No one hovered anywhere in sight. Even the maid seemed to have taken the path around back; she certainly hadn't come in behind Willa. Willa waved her still-smoldering cigar toward the stairs. "Keeps it up there, does she? The dress?"

"My daughter's clothes are a matter for her and her dressmaker." Willa noted the hand that came to rest on the ball newel at the base of the stair-way, effectively barring access to the rest of the house. "Now, I really think it's time for you to leave. Or do I have to call the constables?"

Lifting an eyebrow, Willa tipped her head to look up at him. "I believe it was *you* who asked *me* inside."

"Only to keep you from making a spectacle of us—as well as your-self—outside my gate." He shook his head. "But I'll not be embarrassed into letting you harass Clara."

Willa sighed. "I'm not trying to harass your daughter, sir. I'm trying to help her."

"By making us a laughingstock?"

"No, by getting rid of your ghost."

His face flushed red before blanching. "There's no ghost."

"No?" Rummaging deep into her valise, Willa pulled forth a well-thumbed collection of newsprint. "Then this is a lie?" She handed him the top piece, from a society page in a New York paper: "Upstate Beauty Haunted by President." "And this as well?" The *Boston Herald* didn't have a society page, but that didn't prevent them from printing "Debutante's Dress Draws Presidential Ghost" in a narrow column under the heading "News That's Noteworthy." She didn't bother to pass him the other articles drawn from sources closer to home. Just as well, really. Before she could press him further, Clara Harris's father spun on one heel and threw the pages he held into the front room's fireplace. He stood for a long time, staring into the quick burst of flames while Willa tucked the other bits of newsprint away. "That won't get rid of the ghost you know."

"Get out."

Sighing, Willa picked up her bag and pulled a small card from it. "This is the name of my hotel. My name is on the back. I'll be there until the end of the week." Placing the card on the lowest step of the stairway, she pulled her cloak closer about her and turned to leave.

The swish of quality fabric sliding against itself at the top of the stairs gave her pause. A quick glance upward let her gaze directly into the soft brown eyes of the woman in the newspaper photos. If anything, she was more beautiful in person. The stiff expressions demanded by photography couldn't capture the luminous quality of her skin or the intensity of her gaze. Willa stopped, waited.

The woman's voice, husky as if she hadn't spoken at all that day, was still firm. "Can you make it go away?"

Willa nodded. "Yes. I think so."

"Then, please, come up."

Neither woman looked toward the front room as Willa climbed the stairs.

Like the rest of the house, the bedroom Willa was shown to, Clara's room, was tiny and tidy. Although full of the usual things young ladies seemed to think essential, it still remained an orderly retreat. Willa saw several books close by the bed; a watercolor was taking shape on an easel near the window. Combs and brushes were lined up like soldiers on the dresser. A modest number of cosmetics and toiletries were corraled near the mirror. In all, it was probably more restrained than most debutantes' rooms. Which made the pile of dresses, capes, skirts, and blouses piled atop a corner chair all the more disconcerting. Glancing pointedly at the chaos of hems and lace, Willa said, "I take it the dress isn't among that lot."

Clara shook her head silently before crossing to the far corner of the room to lay her hand against an oaken panel. Clearly newer than the rest, it had, nevertheless, been cut to resemble the other, older wood covering the walls. "I . . . This was a closet. I had it sealed up. I couldn't bear to look at it, but . . . I couldn't bear to destroy it, either."

"Or even give it away?"

Clara shook her head again. The fingers she pressed on the newer section of wood turned white. "No."

Moving into the evening's last rays of light where they fell through Clara's narrow window, Willa glanced outside. "Not even when the ghost first appeared?"

"I'd already had it sealed up by then."

Willa's eyebrow rose slowly. "Really? I don't think that would have stopped me from getting it out again—if it would stop the visitations." She reached out to touch the wood. "But you didn't."

Clara slumped down on the edge of the bed. "I don't even know why I brought it back. It's horrible, really. 'Morbid,' my mother says." Clara shrugged, hands rising and falling softly back to her lap. "I should have thrown it out back in New York. I—I don't know why I didn't."

"Well, it's a relic, isn't it?" Clara frowned and Willa continued. "Blood's the ancient binder. It means something. Even the Catholics believe in the power in their bits and pieces of saints and all, don't they?" Clara's nod was slow. "Lincoln was a fine man, or so I'm told. Wouldn't be unreasonable if you wanted to keep a little piece of that for yourself."

"But it was so horrible!" The woman's voice leapt from hush to frantic wail in just five words. Her eyes turned to gaze on the new wood. "It wasn't just blood." She swallowed hard. "Bits of bone, and—and . . ."

Willa caught one of Clara's hands in her own, squeezed until the girl's eyes gave up their intense scrutiny of the wall to meet her own, and then laid it back in Clara's lap. "You mustn't dwell on that."

"But that's why it's here, isn't it? Why this—this spirit . . ."

"Why this spirit does what? What does it do?"

"It scares me."

"How?"

"It's cold. So very cold." Clara tucked her hands deep in the folds of her skirts, as if to warm them. "There's almost nothing to see, just a . . . a sort of whiteness, a bit of light where there shouldn't be any. Sometimes there are dark holes where eyes might be, mostly just a shape, tall and gaunt. Like the other side, the reverse side, of a shadow. But the cold, the cold is always there." Her voice dropped to nearly nothing. "That cold can walk right through you."

Nodding to herself, Willa lifted her bag onto the bed and began poking through it. "If there was a priest here who was willing to acknowledge a ghost in the first place, you might be able to get him to exorcise this presence of yours. In the absence of such enlightened churchmen, you'll just have to make do with me."

Chalk and twine and bits of dead plants landed on Clara's bed, followed by a full dozen smooth, flat gray stones. While Willa continued to catalog the items she'd need, including a variety of colored candles, a bag of flour, and a pot of ink, Clara Harris fingered the stones. A more perfectly matched set was hard to imagine. Each of these fit exactly in the palm of her hand, and, tossing two of them, one in either hand, Clara couldn't feel any difference in their heft. Turning them over, she discovered that all the stones contained a thin line of some paler, almost white, mineral running through them. Lining them up next to one another, they looked like the playing pieces for some game. "Where did you find these, so many, so alike?"

Willa shrugged as she crouched in the middle of what floor space was available and began drawing a circle with the chalk. "From a stream. I spent quite a few summers looking for them, trying to match them to one another. The woman who taught me her bits of knowledge seemed to think it was important that they come from the 'same bony ground' as me, but I mostly just did what I felt was right and, she didn't ask me too many questions."

Clara grinned. "You mean, like I'm doing?"

"Well, no, but this does take some time to set up."

Quietly then, the two women sat in the bedroom, one tracing out the circles and strange little almost-letters around their edges while the other let the rocks slide through her hands one after the other. Willa was about halfway done when she asked Clara to light a lamp so she could see to finish the job. It was several hours later before the final curlicue was in place.

Willa sat back, rubbed her hands together to ease out the cramps that were only slightly more uncomfortable than the one running the entire length of her back.

Clara leaned forward, tracing the lines with a finger held just a handspan above them. "What does it all mean?"

"Lots of things. Mostly, 'Hey, ghost, get yourself over here where I can catch you.'"

"Really?"

"Well, I could tell you that that symbol there"—she pointed to a square within a double circle—"calls elements of air to itself, including the ether that more knowledgeable women than myself tell me forms the basis for a spirit on this plane." She held a hand above a second marking, this one egg-shaped, and continued. "Or that this one here is the Sigil of Nothingness, which is what we want left in this house." She shrugged. "But, I don't think it would mean much to you. Not really."

"Probably not." Clara's deep brown eyes turned slowly, taking in the walls as if expecting them to do something more than stand there. Which is probably true, Willa thought to herself. "But it will work?"

"I think so. It should, at any rate."

For all Clara's attention to the room around her, she didn't miss Willa's faint shiver as she got to her feet. "Oh, where is my head!" With something to do, the girl was all movement, fairly dancing toward the hallway. "You've been at this for simply ages! You must be hungry—and thirsty." She pulled a shawl from the mess in the chair and dropped it over Willa's shoulders. "You must be simply frozen from sitting down there all this while. Go, sit on the bed. I'll fetch us some tea from downstairs. Gilly always has the kettle on the back of the stove." Before Willa could answer, the young woman was out the door. Her feet made barely a sound on the stairs.

The thought of hot tea was good, and, all things taken together, it was probably just as well that the young woman wouldn't see the very last addition to the Circle of Power that Willa was setting in place. Stones and chalk were one thing, but most people just didn't like the next part.

The short knife she pulled from her skirt pocket wasn't the one she'd normally use to bite into the vein that stood nice and prominent over the knobby bone in her wrist. Silver didn't hold an edge at all, and piercing even her thin skin involved a fair bit of hacking, but anything else risked ruining the efforts she'd already expended on this apparition. Cursing the messy job she was making of her wrist, she gritted her teeth and leaned into the cut until blood, claret red and heavy, oozed up around the blade. She had already coated each stone with blood and set all but three inside the Circle when she heard steps again.

These weren't Clara's light steps, though. Heavy, stumbling, unsteady, they stopped in the doorway and Willa looked up to see the father, florid face telling of too much liquor, wavering in the opening. Ignoring him, she reached for another stone. The blood wouldn't run forever and she certainly didn't want to have to reopen this vein with that knife.

"What— What in the name of God?" Harris reached out to grab the edge of the door frame, missed, and dropped his glass. "W-what are you doing, woman!"

"Trying to save your daughter, Mr. Harris." The second to last stone was in her hands now and she scuttled to the left to set it inside its proscribed space, the small clear area next to the symbol of Air. "So why don't you go off and let me do it?" As usual, the wound was healing over just before she was finished. Exasperated, Willa twisted her wrist sharply and, with her bloody hand, pressed against the veins in her forearm, milking another few drops from the jagged tear. They were dripping down her fingers when she reached for the last stone, the first she'd found all those years ago. Her fingers closed on empty air as pain erupted across her scalp.

"Get out of my house!" Harris's voice roared in her ear as the fingers tangled in her hair yanked her upright. "Get out, get out, get out!"

Her fingers slid over the hand that wrenched her higher and higher, nearly lifting her from the floor. The blood she'd eked out just seconds ago left her hands too slippery to grip. Wrapping both arms around his forearm eased the pressure threatening to tear chunks of hair and flesh from her head, but left her helpless to prevent him from dragging her through the doorway and into the hall. "Let me go! Clara!"

His free hand struck her face and more blood than she could ever have used for the whole ritual exploded from her nose and lips. "Witch, whore!"

The stair rail dug deep into the small of her back, his hand pulled her head farther back with each passing second. If he didn't break her back first, Harris's intent, to throw her brittle old bones out over that twenty-foot drop, was clear. Twisting, scratching, kicking, even biting, did nothing against the six-foot, two-hundred-pound weight inexorably pressing her farther out into empty air.

"Father!" The voice echoed sharply in the stairwell, bouncing off hardwood treads, wooden paneling, the flat hard floor waiting below Willa. "Father, stop!"

"Stay away, girl. Stay away." The steps rushing up the stairs slowed.

"Father, what are you doing?"

"What I ought to have done the first time I saw this creature." Willa gasped as her feet left the ground. Only the rail pressing into her spine kept her from falling.

"But, Father—"

"No!"

Willa's eyes closed as the subtle balance beneath her back began to change. Clara's feet took the stairs two at a time, but there was simply no time. Willa felt the sudden release of pain as his fingers shook themselves free of her hair. Willa knew, intellectually, that the fall took less than seconds, but in that time the dream of a dozen nights played itself out behind her lids once more. Clara, chased by shades of a dead president, slowly curling into the shadows of this house, terror and desperation destroying the gentle features. Clara again, older, married, deliriously happy to finally escape her haunted home, the house her father refused to leave. Clara, older yet, discovering that, in fleeing this terror, she'd flown straight into the arms of evil. Darkness, as real, yet ephemeral, as fog rising off morning water, surrounded Clara's future—a future that Willa was now helpless to change.

Her head struck the floor with a dull *thwap*. Light exploded inside her, flickered, then spiraled down into darkness.

Clara pulled the covers closer to her face. Her breath stilled in her chest as the wisp of white emerged once more from the paler stretch of wall. It paused over the smeared remains of Willa Farraugh's circle, then gusted forward. The scream in Clara's throat died in the sharp cold flooding her room. Pressing her face into the bunched sheets in her hands, she waited. The small pile of stones, still sticky with Willa's blood, rested around her.

"Please, please, please . . ." Her mutter, no spell, but a mantra nonetheless, whispered through stiff lips. For a moment, the chill eased and, ever so slowly, she lifted her head.

All around her, the mist hovered, dancing outside the circle of stones. Hope flared inside her, then died as, with an audible hiss, the bitterly cold air rushed like water over the palest stone, the one Willa hadn't set inside her circle.

Clara screamed into the blankets until the cold stole the sound from her throat.

For those who might not recognize the name Clara Harris, she was indeed a real woman, who, along with others, went to Ford's Theater to see the play *Our American Cousin* on April 14, 1865. Stories about the haunting of Loudon Cottage, her home in upstate New York, began before John Wilkes Booth was caught eleven days after assassinating Lincoln that same night at Ford's Theater. Over the next few years, dozens of mystics, occultists, and the then-chic parapsychologists would attempt to investigate and explain the bizarre happenings that began after the murder. One such investigator, Wilhelmina Fraug, claimed to foresee much misery for the house's occupants—just before slipping on the stairs and falling to her death.

Clara Harris did marry and move out of Loudon Cottage. After years in a marriage that even the most optimistic counselor would term troubled, Clara Harris was murdered by her husband, in front of their three children.

It's been said that Clara Harris's spirit fled back to Loudon Cottage but apparently it had no desire to share its accommodations with Lincoln, choosing instead to haunt the gardens where, from time to time, small piles of smooth stones would be found.

Although stones in occult legend and literature have been used for other purposes, such as divination or weather-witching, Willa's use of stones in "The Stone Sorcerer" is the more traditional, directly relating to motifs of death and spiritual binding. That same relationship is evident in *The Blair Witch Project,* in which piles of stones appear just before the first disappearance. Whatever else Heather, Josh, and Mickey *might* have been doing in that more-questions-asked-than-answered film, we can be pretty sure they weren't casting horoscopes!

The last piece in this section, which is still sung today, dates to 1782 and presents perhaps the most unique use of stones in occult practice.

To Stones Returning

Not for me the flames of burning,
Or the bitter spate of yearning,
For my life in Craft undone.

No, I am to the stones returning.

Think you to spend eternity in hell,

Or purgatory for some undetermined spell?

Not for me those fascinations.

No, I am to the stones returning.

Standing now upon the eternal portal,

Shaved of witless thoughts immortal,

The sentence senseless, not yet done.

No, I am to the stones returning.

Waters stroke and smooth and soothe me,

'Til my present troubles flee,

Stone and bone shall lie together.

I am to the stones returning.

—Corbis Corby

Making the connection between "To Stones Returning" and *The Blair Witch Project* is a long-held belief that witches, sorcerers, or wizards could pass through stone, in a sense become stone, when it suited their purposes. At least two early versions of the Arthurian legend have Merlin zipping across Great Britain through the rock of the island itself, accounting for his ability to appear when needed despite being sighted hundreds of miles away on the same day. Modern neo-paganism carried on this belief in a slightly altered form, suggesting that persons with the right knowledge weren't traveling through Great Britain's bedrock exactly but rather flitting from rock to rock at incredible speed along "ley lines," the metaphysical power lines that some believe were marked by lines of standing stones over large portions of the Continent as well as the British Isles. As a sort of sideline to this belief there was the assumption that a sorcerer or witch powerful enough to travel this mystical road might well be able to lure the innocent into attempting the journey from rock to rock or through the earth itself only to deliberately lose their unwary companion along the way, leaving them trapped, body and soul, inside the stones or ground. The later notion that witches could trap their victims inside stones of a particular shape or color was merely a small step away from the original legends.

In "To Stones Returning," Corbis Corby, not actually a real person but a magical name taken from the Latin for "crow," has been caught practicing witchcraft and sentenced to burn. Not looking forward to that prospect, he decides to skip the wizard-roast by hiding in whatever stones he finds handy. It's not the perfect solution: some legends assert that sorcerers hiding out this way must wait until running water erodes the stones to the point where the wizard can escape. (Which also accounts for the many legends and folktales featuring witches who turned up again and again, usually, as in the case of the Blair Witch, after predictable periods of time.) Still, it beat being burned at the stake!

by children led

Although infants are no longer seen as the "blank slates" early child psychologists presumed they were, the belief, the *need* to believe, in childhood innocence runs deep even today when an eight-year-old boy can calmly confess to knifing both parents because "they grounded me!" The testimony of children has always enjoyed a special place in the justice system, being, for hard to define reasons, weightier than the same testimony given by an adult. Any lawyer can tell you that juries respond positively to children's testimony, accepting evidence from them without raising pesky issues like motive. Only the bravest attorneys want to openly challenge a child witness; such "brow-beating" only alienates juries. "Why would a child lie?" is the unspoken addendum to nearly all statements from children.

The more cynical, of course, ask, "Why not?" Don't children have the same needs as adults, the same desires? Wouldn't a child who enjoyed the limelight, who craved adult attention, adult powers, use adult means to obtain them? Though logic says yes, human beings seem all too anxious to ignore any evidence of the more adult sins in their children. "Not *my* Johnny (or Timmy or Anna or Ling or Juan)!" Enamored as we are of the romantic notion of childhood as an innocent romp, we can't quite seem to envision Ling, Juan, and Johnny sitting around the schoolyard deciding how best to hold up the local convenience store, or talk their way out of drug possession charges—or murder good old Granny who's been holding out on the allowance since catching them trying to barbecue the neighbor's cat. Yet, children have done all those things, and worse.

The Trials at Salem — Briefly

Perhaps the most shameful event in America's occult history, the witch trials in Salem Village, were begun by children. Nine-year-old

Elizabeth Parris and eleven-year-old Abigail Williams began attracting attention in January of 1692—not for anything as esoteric as witchery, but for the bizarre illness that seemed to overtake them.

For several weeks, the girls fainted, convulsed, and screamed obscenities in between long bouts of staring off into space. Soon, other girls of their acquaintance began shaking and screaming. Unable to find a medical cause for their behavior, their doctors determined that the girls must all be the victims of the Devil and his servants, witches.

Not one girl mentioned knowing a witch until the stumped adults brought up the notion for open debate. Shortly thereafter, however, Parris and Williams, along with their friends, were not only accusing residents of Salem Village of witchery but being taken off to other communities to pick out a few witches among strangers, of whom they couldn't possibly have had any firsthand knowledge. Perhaps it was to avoid any more "witch cake," a horrid conglomeration of rye meal and the girls' own urine, believed to make it possible for a witch's victim to identify the witch, but, less than six months after making their first accusation in Salem Village, the girls, at the urging of John Ballard of Andover, were pointing fingers once again and setting off the Andover Witch Hunt.

During the trials in Salem, more than a score of people would be accused, convicted, and executed, often on nothing more than the say-so of the girls. No wonder Martha Carrier, one of the unfortunates so convicted, was recorded as saying, "I am wronged! It is a shameful thing that you should mind these folks that are out of their wits!" Yet "mind" them the courts did.

On May 10, Sarah Osbourne, one of the first women accused, died in prison.

On June 10, Bridget Bishop became the first person officially executed under the Salem witch trials. She was hanged, badly.

July 19 marked the first mass execution. Sarah Good, Sarah Wildes, Susannah Martin, Elizabeth Howe, and Rebecca Nurse were all hanged after, once again, protesting their innocence.

Exactly one month later, on August 19, the next wave of hangings took place. This time, both men and women died: Martha Carrier was joined by John Proctor, John Willard, and the two Georges, George Jacobs and George Burroughs.

On September 19, Giles Corey, who protested his innocence to the point of refusing a trial, was provided with a unique (for the Salem witch trials) form of execution—he was pressed to death.

A few days later, on September 22, women once more made up the majority of those hanged on Gallows Hill when Margaret Scott, Mary Easty (who was released once, then tried and convicted), Alice Parker, Mary Parker, Martha Corey, and Ann Pudeator died alongside Wilmott Redd and Samuel Wardwell.

Small wonder then that in establishing a back history for their fictional New England witch, the directors of *The Blair Witch Project,* Sánchez and Myrick, would portray the inciting incident between Elly Kedward and the community of Blair as accusations and counteraccusations between the alleged witch and the town's children. In the Blair Witch mythos, Elly Kedward attempted to lure several children into her isolated home where she then proceeded to steal their blood. On the basis of their testimony, she was dispossessed of her home and the safety of her settlement, then driven off into the cold of winter to die.

Which is not to imply that the children featured in fairy tales, or witch tales, or even actual occult history, always win. Hansel and Gretel may have pushed their old woman into the oven, but Sarah Churchill, one of the Salem girls who was so busy accusing her neighbors of witchcraft, was also one of those examined by the committee her accusations helped establish.

This next tale, "Witch-Childe," casts children as both victims and accusers, illustrating once again that strange juxtaposition of good and evil/innocence and sin that marks so many American occult tales.

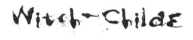

1819

The child wandered idly across the crowded common, unremarkable if not for her unblinking gaze and the plaited leash running from her neck to the hand of a tall man walking behind her. For several minutes, Ruth watched the two progress along the park's paths, noted the child's unswerving steps, which, without a gentle tug on the leash, would have carried her into people and trees, even over the picnic lunches some had spread on the soft grass on this fine Sunday afternoon. As might be expected, Ruth Tate wasn't the only one watching the odd pair. Though few stared as boldly as Ruth, almost everyone the couple passed gaped at them once the man and child had gone by.

On the wide veranda where Ruth stood, the other women had been too engrossed in their talk of babies and recipes to notice a man, even a well-dressed stranger, on the far side of Speyford's spacious common. They stared at her curiously when she asked aloud, "Is the child blind?"

"Whose child?" Veronique Grennard craned her neck but couldn't see over the rail encircling the porch. Relieving herself of the irksome task of unsnarling the leftover scraps of yarn in the project basket by the simple expedient of dumping half of them in the lap of each housemaid, she joined her mistress at the top of the steps to peer across the open park. "Oi! I see." Lifting a hand to shade her eyes, Ronnie squinted. "If she were only blind, would he not lead her by the hand? No, see how she marches? I think perhaps she is simpleminded."

Ruth shrugged. "There's something peculiar about her certainly."

Veronique let her attention wander between the man and the child. "He dresses her well. Do you think she might be his daughter?" The governess tipped her head to one side as she considered her own question, then answered it. "No, I think not."

Neither did Ruth. The man, nearly halfway across the green now, was as dark as the girl was fair, and heavy-boned, whereas the child sometimes appeared ready to float away if not for the leash linking her to him. When the man paused to speak to a woman spreading a cloth in the shade of a live oak, asking directions (if the woman's pointing hand was any indication), the girl walked as far as the cord permitted, continuing to take step after step despite the fact she could go no farther. So intrigued was Ruth by this odd behavior that she didn't notice the woman's outstretched finger jab in their direction several times. Ronnie nudged her employer's hip with her own, then tipped her head ever so slightly in the man's direction. "He's coming over here!"

Startled, Ruth drew herself up and glanced toward the far end of the veranda where her own daughters were dancing their rag dolls about on a braided rug. "Take the girls inside, would you?"

"Of course." Turning her head so only Ruth could catch her expression, she grinned widely. "But, if I must hide away with the children, you must promise to tell me *everything* he says."

Ruth shook her head and smiled as the French girl herded students and maids ahead of her into the house and closed the door firmly. As Matthew had so often commented, the girl *was* a terrible gossip. Fortunately for Lily and Emily, Veronique was also a marvelous teacher and, as she scrupulously avoided gossiping in front of the twins, Matthew was more than willing to put up with Veronique's chatter over supper. And, in all truth, Veronique's most outrageous comments about Speyford's community leaders were all too often accurate.

Composing her face and folding her hands together, Ruth became the image of a well-heeled young physician's wife by the time the man arrived at the bottom of her steps. "Mrs. Tate?"

"Yes, I'm Mrs. Tate. How may I help you? If you're looking for the surgery, I'm afraid it's on the other side of the green."

She was lifting a hand to point toward Matthew's neat office when the man shook his head. "Actually, ma'am, it's not a medical matter that's brought me here, but a personal one. If I might speak with your husband?"

Ruth shrugged lightly. "He's not home at the moment. Would you care to leave your name and an address where he might call on you when he returns?" Ruth wouldn't allow herself to stare at the child, who had once again reached the end of her tether, but it was impossible not to see the girl's repeated attempts to climb the steps, not to hear the toes of her shoes strike the risers again and again.

"Do you expect him back soon?"

"Not before supper. He's visiting for the afternoon." As the man continued to stand there silently as he considered his options, it prompted Ruth to add, "Do you have a card, or a message, you'd like to leave?"

He shook his head. "No, I think it best if I discuss this matter with him directly. I trust I may call again this evening?"

"Of course, sir. My husband only attends the most serious cases on a Sunday, so, barring incident, he should be home all evening."

"Thank you, ma'am." Tugging lightly on the cord, he sketched a brief bow and turned to make his slow way back across the green.

Left to mull over the short meeting, Ruth found her thoughts turning more often to the silent child than to the man. Despite her blank expression, Ruth had caught something, something almost familiar about the girl. Yet, when Veronique bustled back onto the porch, she could find no words to describe the odd feeling and, instead of exploring it further, merely nodded when Ronnie noted, repeatedly, the handsome figure the strange man cut.

Matthew waited on the porch with her that evening, openly eager to see the strange pair for himself. At supper, he'd been nearly as full of questions as Ronnie, who had now decided the man was by far the most attractive gentleman she'd seen in months. Ruth wasn't sure which she'd found more irritating, Ronnie's repeated queries about the man's eye color or Matthew's speculation on the man's probable profession. Her anxiety hadn't faded as the day moved along, and she now found her hands unsteady on the tea things she was laying on the veranda table. She wasn't sure when the decision had been made, but sometime that afternoon she'd resolved that neither the man nor his strange charge need come inside the house.

The man's arrival, seemingly out of the darkness itself, with the child once more attached to him by the leash, startled her. When Matthew started down the steps to greet these peculiar guests, she had to pull back her hand, which had, without her conscious will, lifted to catch his sleeve and hold him back.

In truth, there was nothing overtly threatening about either of them. The little girl, in green velvet with a matching ribbon to hold masses of soft blond curls off her face, stood quietly enough with the man's hand resting on her shoulder. And, Veronique's "mysterious stranger" looked perfectly ordinary when he shook hands with Matthew and offered him his card.

Matthew tipped the rectangle of good paper toward the house, catching just enough light to read it without squinting. "Bartholomew Crowley, Barrister," he read aloud while gesturing the two to join him on the veranda. "Boston. Little out of your way out here."

The man nodded greetings to Ruth before responding. "Some matters are best handled personally, Dr. Tate."

"True enough." Ruth watched her husband's gaze travel over the girl, first with professional curiosity, then more closely, as one might look twice at someone one should recognize. "It must be something very important though, to bring you all this way."

The child's semblance of normalcy disappeared when, at the silent gesture Ruth made for them all to sit, Bartholomew Crowley lifted the girl to the seat of a deep wicker chair. Instead of perching on the edge as her own girls did, their legs just a tad longer than this child's, this girl scuttled backward into the farthest corner and drew her legs up to either side. Leaning forward, her chest flat against her lap, with her arms wrapped about her knees, the girl resembled a frog more than any human child!

Instinctively, Ruth reached to straighten the child's limbs but Crowley stopped her with a single shake of his head. "Rachel . . . Rachel doesn't sit, Mrs. Tate."

"Rachel? Is that her name then?"

"Yes, ma'am." He paused, then shrugged and spread his hands. "Rachel Elspeth Tate."

"Tate!" Matthew crouched to brush the hair back from the girl's face. In that moment, in the two profiles facing one another, Ruth recognized what had nagged her all afternoon: the same thick blond hair, the same slender fingers, the same wide charcoal gray eyes. Ruth's own daughters could look no more like Matthew than this child. When his tentative touches couldn't urge Rachel into a more human pose, he turned his attentions to the barrister. "Perhaps you could tell us just who this child is, and how she came to be in this state."

"Of course, sir, that was, after all, my purpose in bringing her here."

Tea was the least of the social niceties ignored over the next hour as Ruth and Matthew Tate learned that their lives were about to change forever.

Crowley began by pulling a creamy envelope from a pocket inside his coat. He didn't hand it over immediately, choosing to rub his fingers across it as he spoke. "As I said, the child's name is Rachel Tate. She's the legitimately born daughter of Anna and Francis Tate, who I believe was your eldest brother?"

Matthew sank into a chair next to Rachel, waving Crowley to another across from them. "My only brother, my elder by nearly eighteen years."

He shook his head once, then sighed. "I haven't seen him since I was a boy. He went to India before I turned ten, to grow tea or spices or something." His hands pleated, then smoothed one leg of his trousers as he stared down at Rachel. "I suppose I assumed he married, had children. Not because I had specific knowledge that he'd done so, none of the family heard from him after the first few letters home, but because, well, it's what people do, isn't it? Get married, raise families."

"Indeed. He married Anna Montrose, the daughter of one of his neighbors, just a year after his arrival in India, but the marriage was barren for most of that time. I believe there was another child, during the first year of the marriage. I understand it died of one of those tropical fevers." Crowley shifted uneasily. His fingers ran lightly over the envelope, but he continued to hold it as he continued. "About eight years ago, Anna Montrose-Tate's parents died in a house fire. She inherited their property and joined it to her husband's to create one large plantation. Her one remaining relative, an elderly great-aunt who'd been away at the time of the fire, moved into your brother's house almost immediately."

Ruth peered at the child again. "This was before Rachel was born?"

"Yes, the girl will be six three days before Christmas."

Just a year younger than her own girls.

Matthew leaned forward. "Go on."

"Nothing of note appears to have happened between the fire and Rachel's birth two years later. Your brother's business flourished, things

went well. I've inferred from various correspondences that Mrs. Tate's second pregnancy took them all somewhat by surprise, but pleasantly."

Ruth shifted uneasily. "Excuse me, but, does the child understand English? Perhaps I should take her inside while you finish this discussion."

"I'm told by your brother-in-law that her early years were quite unextraordinary, Mrs. Tate. She walked at the usual age, talked at the usual times, had a fairly comprehensive vocabulary, all perfectly normal, perhaps even a bit above average. Rachel had picked up enough of the local lingo to make her needs known to the staff, who couldn't speak even pidgin English." He glanced at the girl who clearly did nothing normally anymore. "To all appearances, however, she no longer comprehends everyday conversations. I doubt anything we say here today will disturb her."

For her part, Ruth was already disturbed. Pulling another chair into the light falling through the windows, she sat next to the girl, idly toying with the leash that still dangled from Rachel's neck. "And why *is* that, Mr. Crowley? Another tropical fever?"

Matthew was shaking his head before the barrister could reply. "Admittedly, this isn't my field, but I've never seen anything like this. She seems perfectly well formed physically"—he glanced again toward Crowley—"leading me to believe the girl suffers from some mental indisposition? An hysteria of some type?"

Bartholomew Crowley reached across and clicked open the small clasp at the base of the girl's throat, letting the leash slip loose. As Ruth coiled it up and set it aside, he took a moment to collect his thoughts. "The area where Francis Tate set up his home is remote. Native groups often launched dirty little raids on one another, but that had never affected the plantation. Three years ago, your brother and his manager were checking new plantings on the Montrose section of the holding when another local argument broke out. By the time he arrived back at the house that evening, it was over." Matthew stiffened in his chair, but said nothing, only waited. "His wife, her aunt, Rachel's nurse, and two native maids were dead. Most of the field workers were run off." He paused again, then continued in a rush. "Rachel was the only living being in the house. Francis Tate found her huddled under a bed in the servants' quarters." He pointed to the girl's present posture. "Much as she's huddling in that chair, I imagine."

Ruth's nails pressed into her palms. "She saw them murdered?"

Crowley swallowed. "Without a doubt."

"My God." Matthew's face blanched. "And she's been like this ever since?"

"No. She doesn't scream now."

For some time, the adults around the table were as quiet as Rachel. Ruth was the first to stir. "He's sent her here to live with us?" The barrister nodded. "Three years later?" Another nod. "Why? If he kept her with him, there, in the house where her mother was murdered, for three years, what could have driven him to send her away now?" Her voice and eyes were steady when she asked, "What haven't you told us yet, Mr. Crowley?"

Crowley pushed the envelope across to Matthew. "Your brother has sent funds to support her. It's a considerable sum. More will be forthcoming at regular intervals and Miss Tate will also inherit her mother's trust in due time."

Matthew tipped his head to one side. "You haven't answered my wife's question."

"Perhaps, if you wrote to your brother, he could provide you with better answers than I."

"That could take months."

"I don't think it's my place—"

"You're here, he's not." Matthew pushed the envelope aside. "Why is my brother sending his child to a man he hasn't seen in twenty-two years?"

"I'm not at liberty to discuss this further, Mr. Tate."

"Not at liberty?" Matthew considered that for a moment. "And if we refuse to take her?" For the first time, the barrister seemed speechless. Matthew leaned forward into the silence. "Mr. Crowley, I can't imagine anything worse than being separated from my own daughters. Evidently my brother can. I think I need to know what that might be."

Bartholomew Crowley sat perfectly still for the space of three deep breaths. "I suppose you do at that." From the same inside pocket, he pulled a locket and handed it over to Ruth. "That was her mother's. Perhaps you could hold on to it for her?"

"She's never going back to India, is she?"

"No."

"Why?"

"This won't make any sense here." He waved toward the neatly trimmed common, taking in the solid homes facing onto the green, the few people still walking the paths beneath the trees. "They—the natives in India—they claim Rachel is a witch."

Matthew half rose from his chair before he realized that Bartholomew Crowley was absolutely serious. Ruth's hand on his shoulder urged him back down before she asked, "Then they hid her under that bed, didn't they? Her mother and the others?"

"Yes."

"And it wasn't a bit of local rebellion, it was Rachel they were after."

"Yes, though neither Francis Tate nor the local law enforcement officials realized that at the time."

Matthew's hand brushed his niece's pale hair. "But she's just a little girl."

"Yes, Mr. Tate. She is."

A shadow fell across the small grouping as Veronique passed by inside the house. Ruth nodded once, to herself, and stood to scoop the limp girl into her arms. "And little girls should be in bed at this hour." Raising her voice, she called for Veronique, then spoke softly to her husband. "No doubt Mr. Crowley will be able to tell us about her routine, her likes and dislikes, her schooling and the rest in the morning. I'll go help Veronique settle her in. That small room next to ours should be perfect." She paused in the doorway to nod to the barrister. "Good night, Mr. Crowley."

A child like Rachel couldn't fail to attract attention. Over those first two years, Ruth learned to ignore the stares, the hushed comments exchanged behind her back, the invisible space she seemed to carry with her whenever she took the girl out in public.

In the beginning, she'd hoped that, as the child progressed, the people of Speyford would eventually accept her. The leash had gone in the trash that first night and, under Ruth's almost constant touch, she no longer walked into people or objects, could sit for some time before beginning to hunch forward, and even, at times, seemed to take note of the few greetings that came her way.

Now, however, Ruth's hopes were satisfied if no one crossed the street to avoid them. If anything, the child drew more frowns, more startled glances than ever. Instead of resting just her hand on Rachel's shoulder, Ruth had taken to walking with her arm around the girl, holding her close to her side. It was harder to manage her parcels, harder to steer her charge along the street, but on those rare days when Rachel's soft cheek pressed deliberately against Ruth's arm or breast, Ruth felt herself well rewarded for the extra effort.

It was in the midst of just such a moment, when Rachel's arm had tightened for mere seconds around Ruth's waist, and a delighted Ruth had hugged her back, that Ruth heard it: ". . . witch-child . . ." Holding Rachel close, Ruth quickly scanned the faces around her. No one had stopped to speak to them. No one's expression betrayed more than the usual disgust, or the embarrassment at being caught staring. More frightening to Ruth than any direct confrontation was the realization that she had no idea which of the citizens surrounding her had whispered in her ear—and she knew them all well.

Gripping the child closer, Ruth spun on her heel, stepped off the pathway onto grass just beginning to turn brown with winter's approach, and headed straight for home.

Ruth waited alone on the veranda for Matthew that night. Unlike Bartholomew Crowley, Ruth never assumed Rachel didn't understand what was said to, or around, her. More often this year than last, Ruth had seen Rachel's glance turn to rest on Matthew when he entered the room. Did the two brothers look alike? Was Rachel seeing a reflection of her own face? Did Matthew's voice bear any resemblance to the girl's father's? Certainly no other man earned Rachel's notice, making Ruth all the more sure that something was beginning to stir behind the blank facade. Not for anything would Ruth risk discussing her foster daughter's past in front of her. So, she shivered on the steps, waiting for Matthew.

His progress along the path was slow. Instead of looking ahead, toward home and her, Matthew stared at the tips of his best shoes as they swept through drifted leaves. With his shoulders slumped under his winter coat, he looked tired. Ruth wished she had something cheerful to share with him instead of her fears. Only when he failed to react to her tale did she recognize the reason for his slow steps.

"You've already heard something of the sort."

He nodded and, dropping his bag on the veranda, pulled her down to sit next to him on the step. "Business has been off for the past month, Ruth. At first I was almost delighted, thinking we'd gotten through the change of season and the harvests without too much accident or illness." He shook his head. "But it wasn't that at all. Seems a certain portion of Speyford's population would rather go to Dr. Andrew Phillips, a ninety-year-old man whose eyes aren't what they used to be, rather than consort with a doctor who harbors a witch." He sighed. "I'm sure that situation won't last forever. Already today I've spent nearly three hours repairing Andrew's botched efforts." Shaking his head, he picked up her hand to lace his fingers between hers. "I just can't understand how it got around, especially after all this time."

Ruth cornered Veronique in the teacher's room immediately after the children were in bed. "Ronnie, how *could* you?"

The usually ebullient young woman stood silent, head down but so rigid it was obvious that guilt wasn't her only, even her prevalent, emotion. It was anger that curled the teacher's hands into tiny fists at her sides. "You don't understand."

"No, I don't." Ruth rubbed a hand across her forehead before wrapping both arms around herself. "It was hard before. It'll be impossible for anyone to accept her now that you've spread that silly story everywhere."

The quick toss of her head that flicked her hair back over her shoulder, that let her roll her eyes and shake her head all at once, was quintessentially Gallic. So, too, was the passionate temperament that allowed Veronique to simultaneously sob and shout. "I am sorry, Madam, but they would not have accepted her anyway!" A smattering of something Ruth couldn't translate fast enough heralded Veronique's change from chastised servant to outraged equal. "You say how could *I?* How could *you?* How could you not hear what they were saying about *you?* About Matthew?" Veronique's lips tightened. "I could not stand it, Madam. To hear them ridicule you, when you have done more for that child than anyone! Sanctimonious prigs!" The Frenchwoman was working herself into a state. Color flared across her cheeks. Her hands shook. "Didn't you realize what they would all think? Bringing a child so like your own into this house? How their dirty little minds would twist and turn looking for sordid explanations?"

Startled by this outburst, Ruth shook her head and sat on the edge of the bed. "What do you mean? Everyone knows Rachel is Matthew's niece."

"Do they? I tell you plainly, Ruth Anne Tate, that no one believes Rachel is the daughter of some conveniently absent brother that no one's ever seen!" Her eyes looked heavenward as she lowered her voice. "What everyone *knows,* Madam, is that Ruth Tate is raising her husband's mistake, that he didn't even have the decency to maintain his bastard somewhere else." Veronique's hands reached to grip Ruth's. "I could not stand to hear such things said of you, or him. At least now, they condemn her for the truth instead of lies." Her hair was working its way forward over her shoulders again, sticking to her warm cheeks. "I am not sorry for speaking the truth to their lies, Ruth. I am only sorry that this must hurt you regardless."

Ruth Tate was quiet for a long time before she squeezed the younger woman's hand once and stood up to leave. "I know you meant well, Ronnie, I just don't know how I'm supposed to raise this child now."

Veronique wrapped an arm around Ruth's waist and hugged her. "It will be all right, you'll see. Speyford isn't some superstitious Indian village."

Ruth smiled for Veronique but, as she closed the door on her way out, she wondered if this time Ronnie had truly grasped the nature of small-town New England. Illegitimacy could be disproved, eventually. This taint, however, was too amorphous to yield so easily to reason.

The first word Rachel spoke in her new home caused Ruth equal amounts of joy and consternation. She'd been with them for eleven years, grown into a physically beautiful young woman under their care, and, if she never did learn to mix easily with people outside their house, she made up for it with a deep attachment to Lily and Emily and a radiant smile that lit her face whenever Ruth or Matthew entered the room.

With the twins grown, Veronique had turned her not inconsiderable attentions to helping Ruth pull Rachel out of whatever mental corner had sheltered the child after her mother's death. Between them, the women kept up a steady stream of conversation, sensations, and physical contact. Small victories began to accumulate: the first time Rachel reached for her own food; her tentative clutching of the doll Lily tucked in her hand whenever she and Emily played house; the moment when Veronique had looked up to find Rachel reaching for the shiny buckle that almost held Veronique's dark curls in order. The morning Ruth arrived in Rachel's room to dress her and found the girl who had once walked into trees now pressing her face to the window to watch the other girls skating in the park, she allowed herself the smallest flush of pride. That very afternoon, she and Veronique had taken her to the small pond and, between them, spent hours pushing her back and forth. Their weariness fled when, on their third fall in as many steps, Rachel laughed.

That evening, Veronique predicted that Rachel, having broken her long silence, would surely soon begin to speak again. In the following weeks, Ruth listened without comment to the low murmurs the young woman made when no one was watching. Still, Rachel's first word, spoken so softly Ruth felt it more as a breath across her neck than heard it as sound, left her shaking.

"Mother."

Later, when hugs and praise sent the young woman dancing off through the house, Veronique shrugged off Ruth's dismay. "What else should she call you? Haven't you raised her? Couldn't she pass as the twins' younger sister?" Veronique smiled. "Haven't you spent as much time with her as with the other two?" At Ruth's sudden sharp cry, she rushed to hold her, rubbing her back and rocking her. "No, no, there, it's not so terrible as all that!" She grinned at her friend and shook her lightly. "No one, including the twins, would claim you could have loved them any more than you have done, even if this needy little thing had *never* come into your lives! Haven't Lily and Emily followed your example? Encouraging Rachel, dragging her into all their games and mischief?" She wiped away the tears clinging to Ruth's lashes. "If she calls you Mother, my friend, then she only speaks the truth."

Matthew clearly shared Veronique's view, insisting that Rachel's first word rated an evening of celebration. That night, at a public dining room, marked another occasion as well. For the first time, Speyford's residents could observe the now-grown woman at their leisure—and they did. And, Veronique, still an outsider despite living in Speyford most of her life, retained an outsider's ability to read subtle nuances in speech and gesture. Before the pudding was served, she knew how wrong she'd been about Speyford, that it really wasn't that different from a group of huddled huts in India. By the time the family rose to go home, Ruth's apprehensions had been soothed, but Veronique's had grown steadily until she was nearly pushing the others ahead of her as they left.

Outside, she tucked her arm through Matthew's, slowing his steps until Ruth and the girls, energized by the excitement of this special treat, had skipped ahead enough to afford them some privacy. Matthew smiled easily as their laughter floated back to him. "It's incredible, isn't it?" He shook his head once. "Things can be so different now."

"Indeed."

Matthew looked down at her. "You don't sound very happy, Veronique."

"Oh, I am happy, Matthew, but I'm not fool enough to believe that because the Tate family is happy, all their neighbors will be happy for them."

"I don't understand."

"No, you wouldn't. You are a nice person. Just as Ruth is a nice person. Which is why I suspect she will be bitterly disappointed over the next few months."

"What do you mean?"

"Because Ruth is happy for her littlest chick, she will expect others to be happy for her as well, to accept the girl at more outings like this one."

"Is that so unreasonable?"

"No, not to reasonable people, but, as your Ruth told me many years ago, when Speyford first chose to look away from Rachel, people aren't always reasonable."

"I still don't see where you're going with this." He stopped to look down at her. "What are you trying to say, that people still won't accept her? What if they don't? The worst that happens is that nothing changes. We can deal with that."

"Ah, but things *have* changed, that much is clear when a girl who was once walked like a dog through town can sit in that same town's fanciest dining room and turn every young man's head." Tucking her hand back through his arm, she drew him along again. "You've enjoyed an enviable position in this community, yes?"

"Well, I suppose so, yes. Things at the practice got rough after Rachel arrived, but we've always made do."

"Exactly."

"Exactly what?"

"Speyford has become very used to being able to point to your troubles, to saying to themselves, 'Yes, he's educated, with a beautiful wife, and a good practice, and has, time after time, shown how much more compassionate than us he is by treating the poor for little or nothing all these years, but it's still *our* children who laugh in the park, *our* daughters who charm.'" Veronique tipped her head to look up at him. "No matter that their lives were small and mean by comparison, the fact that their children could run and play while Rachel stumbled always meant they were at least better off than the Tates." As he was about to protest against her dark view of the world, she shook her head. "You are a doctor, Matthew, and know more than I would ever want to about the state of men's bodies. I, on the other hand, am a gossipy woman. I know more of people's souls than any priest."

She laughed as his rueful grin confirmed his acceptance of that truth but soon turned serious again. "Tonight, Matthew, all that changed.

Though they remain themselves, the small-minded people who snubbed Ruth and took their custom to other physicians, who harbored base prides and prejudices, who whispered and took secret pleasure in your distress, you and yours have changed. You've taken something away from them this evening, Matthew Tate, you and your wife and your witch-child. Don't be surprised if they refuse to forgive that, if they start looking for some way to put you back in the position they need you to fill."

In the months to come, Matthew would look back with gratitude on the insight shared by the gossipy little Frenchwoman.

The first incident was so small Ruth barely took notice of it. All children drew messages in the snow and on frosted windowpanes. Emily and Lily, young women with beaux coming to call, could still be coaxed by the deepest snowdrifts and Rachel's increasingly vocal entreaties to fall back and swing their arms, leaving snow angels in their wake. So, when Ruth saw the stars scratched in the lacy tracery of ice coating Rachel's window, she smiled and continued to tidy the room, making the bed, thinking little of the fact that her seventeen-year-old niece was still entranced by such things. Despite the rapid strides Rachel was making, she remained a child in many ways.

It wasn't until she was leaving and turned to make a final survey of the room that she realized there was something wrong. From the doorway,

Ruth's new line of sight allowed the dark wall of the shed outside to form a backdrop for the white outlines, making the figures that much more easy to see. Instead of the usual stars that Rachel had drawn for several years now, with a single point at the top, these stood topsy-turvy, with one point down and two above. Moving closer to confirm her observation, Ruth realized that Rachel couldn't have etched these outlines at all—they were on the *outside* of the glass.

With Ronnie's help and a bucket of boiled water, Ruth erased the childish symbols of the occult from her foster daughter's window and said nothing to her husband.

It was impossible to hide the next episode, less than a week later, especially as several of their neighbors were already standing and pointing when Matthew stepped outside to discover the next set of stars. No doctor could mistake the red fluid forming three brilliant red inverted pentagrams for anything other than blood. Steam rose gently from the snow. The stars sank deeper under their own heat. Without a word, he began clearing the snow, carting it away to throw over an embankment at the end of the property. Ruth watched from the veranda. Some of those gathered on the street helped Matthew scoop the stained snow into the cart, others made no attempt to lower their voices as they reminded anyone who would listen that only one person in Speyford was known to have been involved in demonic matters and that person lived in the Tate house.

Inside, Veronique lured Rachel away from the front windows with the promise of warm chocolate in the kitchen.

When he was done, Matthew Tate walked directly through the crowd gathered in front of his house, murmured a good-day to those he recognized, and made his way to the office across the common as usual.

Veronique was packing Rachel's clothes into a trunk in the front room, much to the young woman's delight, when Matthew arrived home well before sunset. High color stained his pale face. His hands shook as he set his bag beside the door and shrugged out of his coat.

"Where are Emily and Lily?"

Ruth, arriving from the kitchen with tea on a tray, stopped on the threshold. Her gaze traveled from his face to the clock and back. "What's happened?"

"Nothing."

"I don't understand."

"No. Thing. Nothing." He batted snow off the shoulders of his coat with only slightly less energy than he'd have brushed off snakes. "With the exception of old Phillip Potts, who lives so far out of town he's in a different season than the rest of us, and young Maxwell, I haven't seen a single soul all day." He raked his fingers through his hair. "When it became obvious that none of our scheduled patients were going to appear, I sent my trainee home. He was itching to get out of there anyway—not that I blame him."

"I see." Laying the tray next to his usual chair, she reached for his scarf and gloves. "The tea is hot. Sit while Ronnie gathers up the last few things." To Rachel, she added, "Why don't you run along and help Veronique, all right, love?"

Though her vocabulary of spoken words was growing quickly, bouts of shyness kept Rachel silent from time to time. Still, she nodded and smiled before following her teacher from the room.

Ruth sank into the chair next to Matthew's and sighed. "It's all an adventure to her, thank God."

Matthew gestured toward the trunks. "What's all this? And where are the twins?"

"At the post office. I've written to Mr. Crowley, they're mailing it for me."

He almost grinned as he stretched his legs out in front of him and sank back into the chair. "I should have known you wouldn't spend the day cringing at home. So what have you sent to Mr. Crowley and why are you packing up our youngest child?" He lifted an eyebrow. "I assume you've not decided to ship her off to India because of a few poorly executed symbols in the snow?"

She smiled back at him. "Hardly. But, it did occur to me that, with Rachel coming into her mother's money next month, it might be a good time to visit Boston."

"Give this latest foolishness time to get lost in the next great Speyford scandal, you mean?"

"Something like that."

"Can I assume that the twins approve of this plan?"

"Completely. Lily was mooning about a little at the thought of being away from her young man, but Emily's suggestion, that distance and absence might make his heart grow fonder, brought her around fairly quickly." She paused. "And, who knows, perhaps being forced to choose between Dr. Phillips's shaky hands and that young student's inexperience will make your patients a little more grateful as well."

"Perhaps." Fixing himself a cup of tea, he asked, "And when did you plan to embark on this great exodus?"

"Within the next few days. It'll take us that long to close up the house and the office, but I don't want to linger." Taking a cup for herself, she added, "I've asked Mr. Crowley to rent a house for us until spring."

"That long?"

She nodded. "I'd like Rachel to see some of the schools they have there, and you said that colleague of yours . . . ?"

"Martin Crawford?"

"Yes, Dr. Crawford. You said he's had success with hysteria cases before?"

"Certainly, but, darling, I'm sure he couldn't do any more for Rachel than your own love and care are accomplishing."

"That's kind of you, Matthew, but I'd like to see him anyway. Just to be sure."

"That's hardly going to take us three months, though."

Ruth fell silent for a long time before responding. "I've also asked Mr. Crowley to write to Francis."

"What! Why?"

"It's not right that Rachel has no memories of her own mother, that she thinks of the faces in that locket as nothing more than pretty decorations, that Francis has no idea how wonderful she is." Her eyes were steady as they met her husband's. "I've asked Mr. Crowley to suggest to Francis, in the strongest possible terms, that his daughter needs him. I don't know how long it takes to travel from India to New England, but I imagine three months is well within reason."

"Oh, Ruth, are you sure that's wise? She's just starting to really come around. . . ."

"No, I'm not sure. Since I saw that blood all over our yard, Matthew, I'm not sure of nearly as many things today as I was yesterday." She blew softly over the surface of her tea. "Yet, I can't help thinking that if Rachel's father were more than . . . more than the mysterious brother that no one has ever seen, if people could see that Rachel has a real father, a father like everyone else's, just farther away, I can't help but believe that would make such a difference to their perception of her." She sipped carefully. "It has to."

They sat quietly together for some time, watching Rachel spin from room to room with her arms full of clothes. During one of the periods when they were alone once again, Matthew asked, "What would you have done if I refused to go?"

"Why, Matthew Tate, if I don't know you better than that by now, I wouldn't be much of a wife, would I?"

As she sipped her tea, the twins arrived, full of excited chatter about their upcoming trip. Lily nearly danced as she described her beau's response to the news. "He was so completely miserable! It was marvelous, Mother, absolutely brilliant!"

Emily laughed at that seemingly contradictory statement before adding, "And Prentice Hume is absolutely green with envy! Her mother has been promising to take her to Boston for nearly a year. I can't believe we'll get there before her!" When Veronique and Rachel returned with the last of Rachel's things, Emily caught her startled cousin in her arms and squeezed her. "Thank you, thank you, thank you! Thank you for going off to get hideously wealthy and letting me and Lil come along with you!"

Clearly Rachel hadn't grasped everything Emily had said, but her quick, "You're very welcome," set the entire family laughing.

Anyone watching the scene from the street as the three beautiful young women rushed about the house under the tolerant eyes of their parents and governess would never have guessed that any shadow had ever touched these lives.

It was a scene to inspire envy and, just two days later, Veronique would wonder if there hadn't been someone watching that evening, someone nursing a powerful fear and hatred for one of those young women.

❧　　❧　　❧

Morning dawned bright, revealing a rare marvel. Ropes of lacy flakes, built on the slenderest base, single stands of hanging moss, or nothing but their own delicate edges, spanned the spaces between branches. Undisturbed by any breath of wind, a few even dangled precariously between the common's ranked oaks. Garlands falling under their own weight sparkled as they spun. Everywhere, children raced between the old trunks, their excited shouts bringing parents to the windows and porches.

Rachel had to be reminded, twice, to put on her mittens before racing outside to run through their own garden. Lily and Emily, wrapped in a single huge shawl, watched her from the steps as she reached to touch the nearest loop of flakes, laughed at her cry of dismay when the whole strand reverted to individual stars and fell around her. Ruth managed to keep a straight face when the woman-child shoved her hands deep into her skirt pockets before approaching the next delicate formation. They stayed there as Rachel gravely inspected each and every tree. Ruth slipped forward to share the shawl with her daughters while Veronique declared herself more interested in hot chocolate than snow and headed back inside to start the kettle boiling. Leaving his women-folk to watch Rachel, Matthew voiced a desire for the less decadent pleasure of a cup of tea. "If Ronnie can spare me a cup of water?"

The most extravagant snow figures hung in the trees farthest from the house, closest to the laughing children racing wildly across the park. Rachel stood beneath one when a group of those children, five or six girls in bright coats and caps, burst onto the pathway. They stared at one another for long moments, neither Rachel nor the children saying anything, until the rising sun stroked the dangling streamers of snow. With an almost audible *pouff,* they disintegrated, falling like a miniature blizzard to coat everyone below. Mouths opened in silent O's, lashes blinked madly to dislodge the flakes tangled among them. With a single breath, Rachel and the children squealed at the cold slivers drifting down their necks. Shaking their hair, they laughed together before the others turned to race back onto the common.

Almost as an afterthought, the oldest of them, a dark-haired girl-child dressed in brilliant red, paused to beckon Rachel along the path. Rachel's eyes widened. Her expression when she looked back over her shoulder, equal fright and excitement, left Ruth clutching Lily's hand beneath the shawl's folds. Emily's voice drifted softly over their shoulders. "Just nod, Mother."

Lily's hand squeezed her back, "And *breathe.*"

Ruth's head jerked twice, though it's doubtful Rachel saw the second movement.

Snow flying behind them, Rachel and the others flitted through the trees.

When Ruth wanted to step closer to the porch rail, Emily pulled the shawl free to drop it around Lily's shoulders and tug her mother toward the house. "Let her be. What harm can she come to in full view of half the town? Come inside, Lily will keep an eye on her."

For nearly an hour, Lily wandered from the steps to the front door, passing on the children's every move, delighting in Rachel's unexpected accuracy as a snowball fight developed, crowing loudly at each of her foster sister's hits. "Oh, Mother, you should see her!" When Rachel should have returned to the porch, Lily shooed her back inside. "No, don't! She's doing so well! You'll only distract her."

Despite her numerous treks along the veranda, Lily was more than glad when Emily waved her to the doorway and offered a cup of hot chocolate, one of the many sins Veronique had insisted on passing along to the Tate women. The heat from the doorway warming her outsides and the heat from the chocolate warming her insides could have set Lily's head nodding if not for the occasional chilly gust edging under her skirts and over her feet. Veronique, on the other hand, looked positively flushed as she dragged the last of her trunks into the foyer, stacking it next to the impressive pile that would accompany the family. Fanning herself with one hand, she came to lean against the doorway.

"We should trade places, yes? You come inside, I will watch our most accurate snowball thrower while I cool off." Tugging the shawl from her charge's shoulders, she squinted into the bright morning to ask, "Where *are* the children?"

"Why, they're just there—" She shifted her cup to the other hand to point, then realized they were nowhere in sight.

Veronique's hand gripped her shoulder. "Where?"

"I-I don't know." Her voice rose in quick jerks. "I . . . They were right there just a moment ago!"

It took them nearly an hour to sort out the footprints, eliminating solitary tracks and those obviously belonging to grown men, before settling into a ground-covering half-trot along the only path left them, a mishmash of mostly small prints leading away from the common, away from town. Emily and Lily, younger, but still dressed in their indoor shoes, were falling behind the adults who'd donned sturdier footwear in anticipation of a morning spent moving luggage.

The twins' clear voices carried easily through the frosty air, but despite their numerous shouts, no one responded. Veronique and the Tates didn't waste their breath once they left the edges of Speyford township behind them. They'd called as loudly as the girls at first; not so much as the twitch of a curtain had met their calls, not a single neighbor had shouted back to ask what was wrong. Lips now pressed tightly together, the three pushed their way along the overgrown trail which eventually would lead them to the riverside quays and piers that winter ice routinely shut down.

"They're just trying to scare her, scare us." It was the third time Matthew had said that since they stepped on the trail in the wake of little footprints. "They're only children, after all."

Ruth ignored him and picked up her pace, nearly running behind him, with Veronique close on her heels.

They'd watched, those children waiting until Rachel was unobserved for just those few moments. Those children had done that. The premeditation, by children, left Ruth breathless, unable to cry out. Matthew's fingers closed over her shoulder, pulled her faster along the path as he looked left and right for footsteps in the snow to either side.

It was Veronique who pulled them up to point at the tracks directly in front of them. "See? There, they drag."

They did. Though at times trampled by more prints, a clear pair of long streaks ran steadily ahead. Matthew frowned. "But she's so much bigger than they are."

"And they are so many more than her," Ruth responded shortly before picking up her skirts and running ahead. She found the first spot of brilliant red, then the spray of tiny droplets, just a few yards ahead. Bursting from the trees into the maze of tiny shacks and shanties lining the river, Ruth ran through more of the still-warm red beads without stopping, but she froze when the trail of sloppy prints led to the end of the community pier.

Matthew's hand gripped hers again, tugging her back into the meager shadows between buildings. Neither took their eyes from Rachel, who stood at the very edge of the icy dock, facing her tormentors, her back to the swiftly flowing water, her gaze fixed on the oldest of the girls blocking her way back to shore. Blood trickled from her lip; it had frozen in her hair, been smeared across her clothes. The group had grown since they'd seen them playing on the common. Over a dozen bodies milled about on the wharf, their group attention fixed on Rachel. As Matthew and Ruth watched, Rachel pulled one hand free of her stained mitten to press just below the swelling lip. It came away red. Rachel stared at the blood, seemingly oblivious to the faces pressing toward her.

A rough pole, nothing more than a striped branch, really, flicked out of that circle of rustling, giggling children to slap home against Rachel's hand. The sharp *snick* accompanying the blow registered but quickly became unimportant as Rachel wavered, unbalanced, for long seconds before finally pulling herself back from a fall that had seemed almost inevitable. Matthew's grip on her hand tightened, but Ruth hadn't moved so much as an inch, holding her breath, as Rachel's one sound hand flailed against open air before finding, almost by accident, the lone post supporting the loading wench. The stick flicked out again, missed by inches, allowing its victim precious moments to find some equilibrium.

Ruth felt Matthew's breath against her cheek as he bent to whisper quick instructions. "We can't rush out there. She'll be pushed into the water." She nodded her understanding, not taking her gaze from her foster daughter's face. "I'll work my way around, to the downstream side of the pier. I see some heavy lines hanging there." He pointed. "If all else fails, I may be able to pull her from the river."

Veronique shivered beside her mistress; her teeth chattered softly when she spoke. "I-I'll go back, tell the girls to be silent. With five of us, we might be able to frighten them off."

Ruth was shaking her head even as Ronnie took to her heels, back the way they'd come. "It won't work, Matthew, they're as trapped on that wharf as Rachel. We can't approach them without blocking off this end."

Even as she watched, the semicircle of bodies facing Rachel edged forward. Nervous laughter, sharp squeals, the echoes of wordless taunts overlapped and floated back to them. Rachel didn't move, she had nowhere to go. Already, her heels touched the last board in the dock's surface.

Without a word, Matthew pulled off his heavy coat and the scarf that had been Rachel's first knitting effort, and began unbuttoning his shirt as well.

"What are you doing?"

"If I can't drag Rachel back through them, I'll have to take her off the end." His shirt fell to the ground as he crouched to work the laces of his boots free. "The water will be cold, but . . ."

With his head down, eyes and fingers seeking the uncooperative knots, he didn't see the next surge of bodies on the dock, didn't realize, as Ruth did, that it had been *away* from Rachel. Edging forward, she squinted into the brilliant light, and frowned. Her own voice was a whisper when she asked, "What's she saying?"

His fingers continued working the laces, but he looked up. Frowning, he shook his head. "I can't hear it, can you?"

Ruth inched forward, then froze as an angry rumble filtered through the group on the wharf. Softly at first, Rachel's voice carried, but even when the sounds became louder, distinct, Ruth couldn't make out the words, couldn't tell where one ended and another started. She shook her head. "I don't understand."

Matthew, stripped down to socks, pants, and undershirt, shivered beside her, but he tipped his head to one side as Rachel's voice rose even further, much higher than necessary to simply be heard over the mutters of her attackers. "It's not English."

"Not English?"

"I don't know which one, but I'd bet our last breath that it's some Indian dialect."

"Something from before she came here?" Ruth's eyes widened, "But I didn't think she remembered any of that."

"Evidently she's remembered something."

Rachel took a single step forward, still staring at the tallest of the girls, and once again lifted her hand to her lips. This time, when the blood had trickled over her fingers, she didn't stop to stare at it. With a single, decisive movement, she pressed forward again, her hand snapping forward, sprinkling blood across that pale face, sending the others reeling backward. Ruth heard the first cry, of fear, not anger. It was soon joined by another, and another, as Rachel sent droplets of her own blood back at them and her voice rose even higher, piercing, strident.

The first child to break and run never looked back. She was halfway past the Tates before she saw them and, even then, never slowed. Ruth dimly recognized Prentice Hume's youngest sister, Estelle, but made no move to stop her—or the others who, blood-spattered, quickly followed.

Rachel stepped forward again and her hands rose to sculpt strange shapes in the air. With several feet of wharf behind her, her voice edging into a scream, and blood flicking from her fingertips, she pressed into the tight knot of her remaining tormentors, reaching for the girl who'd asked her to play.

Ruth forced her hands down to her sides, fought the growing urge to cover her ears, to block out the sibilant hisses and crooning cries coming from her foster daughter's mouth. Instead, she gripped Matthew and eased forward. "There's only a few of them now. Come on."

He nodded once and strode ahead. The first child he touched, one of only four remaining, screamed under his hand. He smelled the sharp, distinct odor of urine as the dark-haired girl, no more than ten or eleven years old, wrenched herself free and ran. Ruth ground her teeth, her lips formed a single hard line as she pushed a blond boy aside and reached for Rachel. Her fingers missed by scant inches. Rachel, ignoring both her parents, moved away, toward the last children.

Only the girl in red and a small, terrified boy, caught in the girl's hands and held between her and Rachel, stood between the Tates and their foster daughter, but neither adult tried to lay hands on any of them. Rachel's fingers, still tinged with blood, hovered inches from her adversary's cheek. The boy shook between them, his eyes locked on the woman he'd moments ago called "witch" without any understanding of the word's true meaning. Almost negligently, Rachel's injured hand brushed him aside. Whimpering, he dropped to the icy boards and covered his ears.

Lying there, legs pulled forward as his body pressed itself against the dock, he looked almost like a frog.

The strange words flowed around them, louder, louder, until Ruth's own hands lifted to block her ears. From the corner of her eye, she saw Matthew do the same. Gwenyth, she thought, as Rachel's hand swept toward the girl's brow. That was this girl's name. Gwenyth. At Rachel's touch, Gwenyth's eyes closed and her mouth opened. A wail escaped, soared louder even than Rachel's chanting, to disappear in some range higher than any of them could possibly hear. Rachel fell silent; the child fell to the ground beside the boy.

For long seconds, the silence surrounding the three Tates felt solid, something to leave them deafened and mute. Ruth opened her mouth but found no words. Matthew dropped to one knee, felt for pulses in the two children lying there. Both women saw the relief rising in his face, but neither heard the other's next breath. Wind moved the trees behind them, but no whisper of branches reached them. The river flowed by, but the slap of tiny wavelets against the wharf's pilings was swallowed up in the dead stillness that wrapped itself around them. In utter silence, Ruth groped her way forward, touched Rachel, and pulled her gently into her arms. Rachel's first sob fell into the hollow of Ruth's throat, a soft puff of air, but Rachel heard it.

Sound rushed back: Rachel's "Auntie Montrose . . . ," the choking cries Matthew tried to hide from them as he stood and swept them both close, the clatter of totally impractical shoes as Emily and Lily raced along the dock, the soft snore of a young boy who still sprawled at their feet, his arms and legs splayed to either side, his cheek resting against the ice, the soft words of a French governess who paused to retrieve coat, scarf, and shoes: "So it was the *great-aunt,* not the child. *C'est bon.*"

Nursery Tales

All witch tales contain elements of duality, usually a conflicting duality, but nowhere is that more true than in those tales pairing witches and children. Although children were presumed innocent of all occult knowledge, their rhymes and songs frequently proved they were, in the context of their times, quite knowledgeable.

Among those ditties were charms, wards against evil, and tips for staying out of trouble should they happen to encounter a witch, as this small representative collection shows:

> *Ask me my name,*
> *'Tis pudding and tame.*
> *Ask me again,*
> *I'll tell you the same!*

According to almost all cultures, names have considerable power, and entrusting your true name to a witch was the height of foolishness. Every well-educated child of the colonial period knew that, and through rhymes like "Pudding and Tame" were constantly reminded of their lessons.

And how might children remember all the ways of spotting a witch and thereby avoid giving a witch their name? Why, "The Knowing" provided all those answers:

The Knowing

Does she touch you with her toes,
You've the knowing of a witch.
Does she lead you by the nose,
You've the knowing of a witch.

Does she offer you a sweet,
You've the knowing of a witch.
Does she float up off her feet,
You've the knowing of a witch.

Does she play with a black cat,
You've the knowing of a witch.
Does she hide baldness 'neath her hat,
You've the knowing of a witch.

Does she fear to touch the Bible,
You've the knowing of a witch.

Right: "Looking twice upon your cow" has a more explicit meaning than might be apparent at first glance. Rural folklore postulated that extra limbs or heads were the direct result of a witch's attentions, attentions which, almost by definition, had to be in person. This gives a whole new meaning to the notion of "minding your own business"!

Does she no work, so if she's idle,
You've the knowing of a witch.

Does she touch you with a charm,
You've the knowing of a witch.
Does she take life from your arm,
You've the knowing of a witch.

Does she feed you soured milk,
You've the knowing of a witch.
Does she share you with her ilk,
You've the knowing of a witch.

Does she press fingers to your brow,
You've the knowing of a witch.
Does she look twice upon your cow,
You've the knowing of a witch.

Does she fear the Sacred Light,
You've the knowing of a witch.
Does she cleave then to the night,
You've the knowing of a witch.

Does she try to take a hair,
You've the knowing of a witch.

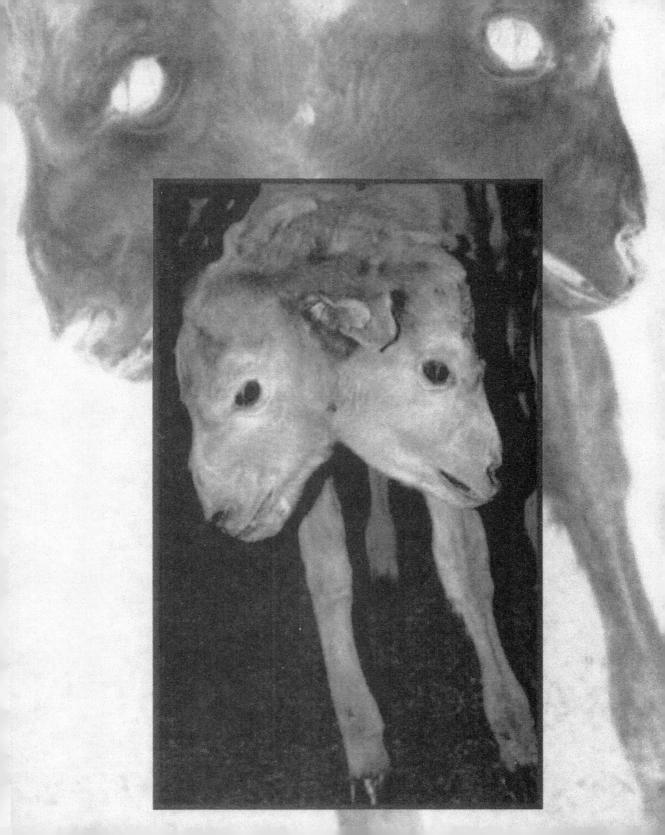

Does she breathe in you foul air,
You've the knowing of a witch.

You've the knowing of a witch!

But suppose the child was already under the influence of a witch? What then? According to a holdover tradition in Newfoundland, a country that has New England ties older than its present association with Canada, adding the following verse to any standard Christian prayer (the irony of mixing Christian mysticism and occult mysticism wasn't wasted on these folk) would invariably do the trick:

Spirits, here, ere end of night,
Reverse my past, undo my plight.
I meant no harm!
With Thee I'll treat,
For my future, once so sweet!

they left their mark

The odd bump in the night, a touch of cold sliding down your back, or a deep groaning behind the bed can all be dismissed, at least once in a while, as something for which there's a "logical explanation." The house settling, a drafty window, and old plumbing are the usual favorites. Then there are events, physical happenings, undeniably real, which, despite the most thorough investigations, continue to defy explanation while simultaneously leaving behind the sort of hard evidence that makes those same events so difficult to dismiss. Perhaps that's why all the best witch stories incorporate some solid, substantial evidence for the existence of that tale's witch.

In *The Blair Witch Project,* everything had an explanation—until Heather found a tiny bundle of *something.* Was it Josh's teeth? His noisy tongue, perhaps? Whatever it was, it was gory and it was, undoubtedly, tied up in the remains of Josh's ugly shirt. Sounds in the night might well be "crazed rednecks." Their unending circular travel might be the result of Heather's inability to read a map. And, maybe, just maybe, they managed to set up a tent dead center among a bunch of rock piles. But there were no mights or maybes capable of dropping that icky little bundle directly in front of their tent entrance without something spooky goin' on!

It's that bit of solid evidence, unexplainable in terms of known reality, that can take a seemingly prosaic tale and launch it into the realm of the occult. In another film, *The Golden Child,* Eddie Murphy's character is told, repeatedly, that the situation in which he's about to become involved reeks of magic and mysticism, but he doesn't believe it, attributing the string of odd events he encounters to the questionable mental status of the other people he meets. He's even ready to believe he's just had the most vivid dream of his life—until he discovers that an injury encountered in the "dream" has left real scars. In another era, the medieval period for example, tiny bits of physical evidence, even those wrapped in a truly hideous shirt, might well have been termed "relics," corporeal links to the unexplained.

If you're in the camp that believes those were really Josh's teeth (which is certainly implied in *The Blair Witch Project Dossier*), you might well find elements of these next few tales familiar. The belief that physical objects, whether inert items that just happen to be present at powerful emotional events or the actual remains of human beings, not only hold echoes of the past but also affect the present or the future is surprisingly global. Christians have a tendency to associate their relics with saints, but older beliefs and superstitions also find expression in modern practice. New parents of today often keep the first lock of hair from their child's first haircut simply as a memento, but the custom's roots are firmly grounded in the occult belief that hair clippings are powerful connections to the hair's owner. Many "sympathetic rituals" required something personal be included in the preparation, and hair was second only to blood in fulfilling that aspect of the magical working. A fourteenth-century letter makes reference to a woman's maid burning the strands of hair taken from her mistress's comb so an enemy could "make no trouble" with them. Nail clippings and, of course, teeth were likewise handled with considerable care. Baby teeth might well be incorporated into a poppet if those figurines were common in the area or, failing that, buried in a remote location. There's even a link between the modern-day conception of the tooth fairy and the "granny witch," who might for some token consideration remove the "essence" of the child from the teeth so they could be safely disposed of later.

Any number of occult folktales begin with some wise auntie being asked to cast a love spell or curse an enemy. In the vast majority, the auntie then nods sagely, asks the petitioner to come up with something belonging to the object of the spell, and suggests that a hair or spot of blood would work so much better than, for example, their lost left glove. "The Bedlam Witch," which dates to the early 1700s in the Carolinas, where it is still told on Halloween, is one of the few tales that turns the tables on a witch.

The Bedlam Witch

Increase Dwyer set Tilla's skin to itchin' and her hair to risin'. And, he didn't have to do much of anything to leave her sputtering like a wet chicken either, not really. Once, he complained that her face should be kept inside of a morning as the sight of it would surely rob any decent man of his appetite for breakfast. Another time, he allowed that perhaps she wasn't as ugly as all that—if you only had to look at her while standing at the bottom of a mine shaft handy about midnight on a moonless night. That really got her in a twitter. Threatened to powwow his wife for that one, she did. 'Course, that only sent Increase into gales of laughter, saying if he had to wait for one of Tilla's hexings to do anything, he'd be an old man and his wife long dead.

I ain't never seen Tilla so mad as that day. And, even though Increase didn't seem too worried, I got to tell ya, I was feeling a smidge uncomfortable when she stomped out of Glover's General. Got the hell out of her way, I did. Yup. I mean, I hadn't seen any of Auntie Tilla's powwowing do anything really awful to no one, not ever, but, with them powwow women, you just can't be sure, can you?

Anyway, Tilla took to staying well clear of Increase after that. She'd mutter under her breath if she saw him coming down the street or something, but, to him directly, she never said a word that I know anything about. He'd sing out loud if he saw her, though, make a right show of himself, get Tilla good and red in the face. Once, when I was sweeping up in front of the General, I heard what she was muttering and it didn't sound like anything I'd want happening to me—even if'n I didn't quite cotton to everything she was sayin'.

May your flame sputter, like a cinder on the hearth,
May you dry up like dung alongside the street,
May your throat burn and never be doused,
May your nether parts shrink and shrivel,
And may all that's yours be made smaller than an imit.

Leastways, that's pretty much the way I remember it. Could have some of them lines in the wrong order, but you get the idea. She wanted the absolute worst to befall Increase, no doubt about it. And she didn't mind who knew as that was the way she felt either. Told Pastor Gather he could stop worrying about Increase's soul, she already had plans for it! Pastor

Gather, he told her right off, right there in the middle of the street. He said a lot of stuff about playing with powers what shouldn't be touched by no God-fearing woman, but Tilla just laughed at him. Then he called her a "whore of Babylon." Now, I know Tilla done be a lot of things in her time, but I know she wasn't no whore, not of any place. Fact, I doubt Tilla even knew where Babylon was! It was 'round about then that she got up some horse droppings from right there in front of the General and flung them at Pastor Gather. Caused a fine bunch of people to congregate, that did.

Now, some folks will tell you that it was that run-in with Pastor Gather that started all the rest of the trouble, but, like I said, I was outside there sweeping up and that's a mighty big porch so I was at it quite a while. I watched Pastor Gather hustling off to change his coat and I watched Tilla lean against the porch rail for a bit after he was gone. She was just shaking her head, sort of chuckling from time to time. I figure she would get to thinking about how Pastor Gather looked with all that horse shit over him and that's what would get her giggling. Some people claimed that she never got over her fight with the Pastor, and that's what caused her ghost to go a'walking about on its own, but they didn't see her up close like I did afterward. I think Tilla let that all go fairly quickly seeing as she figured she'd sort of had the last word. No, I think the thing that got her going was a quiet sort of encounter with Increase Dwyer.

She was just about finished with her chuckling, had asked me to fetch her out a glass of water, when Increase came by looking for some seed catalogs from Mr. Glover. I don't know what he said to her out there on the porch, but she was all shaking when I came back out. She didn't say nothing, though. I gave her the water and was going to wait about a bit, make sure nothing too out of hand happened on Mr. Glover's porch, but Mr. Dwyer sent me inside for the catalogs. He buys a good bit of seed from them catalogs so I figured I best not lose Mr. Glover a sale. I didn't think I'd be inside that long, and I wasn't, but it must have been time enough for Mr. Dwyer to get in a few more cracks at Auntie Tilla. By the time I came back out, she was muttering more of the "shrinking and shriveling" bits and flicking water at him out of the cup I'd given her. He ducked, just when she threw the rest of that cupful at him. It flew right over his shoulder and all over the porch steps. Increase just laughed some more and took the catalog, flicking his own fingers back at her. You could tell from the way his fingers was waving all over that he was just making fun of her, not really trying to powwow her or anything, so I wasn't really expecting anything bad to happen just then. Mostly I was glad to see Auntie Tilla stomping off. Guess I figured that powwowing only worked if you meant it to, not just 'cause you pretended to do it.

Which just goes to show you that I could be wrong. I mean, I still think what happened next was all because of her and Increase Dwyer, but I suppose it could have had something to do with her throwing horse droppings at the Pastor.

Anyway, she was stomping off and I was starting to breathe a bit easier when, all of a sudden, I hear her yell out real loud, just once. I turned quick like, and I saw her foot come out from under her on the steps, just about where I figure that water must have landed, but I wasn't quick enough to catch her. Even Increase made a jump for her, but he couldn't get there any faster than I could.

Auntie Tilla's feet went up and her head came down, sharp like, on the edge of the steps. Gave her face a real wallop. Before she fell, she wasn't quite as ugly as Increase used to say, but after that, well, she didn't look any better for smacking her face off Mr. Glover's front steps. Broke her nose, bled all over the place, split her lip open, knocked out at least one tooth. Mr. Jones, the undertaker, said it was all right that she died real quick from breaking her neck, said that if she hadn't died quick, she'd have looked even worse with all the bleeding. As it was, with her nose all drove over flat on one cheek and everything, she looked pretty bad. I think that's why so many people come to see her laid out.

Hundreds of people turned up just before the funeral. People from as far away as Raleigh came. Now, most of 'em didn't actually stay for the sermonizing. Other than myself and Mr. Glover, the undertaker, the preacher, who looked to go on forever on account of it being Auntie Tilla and she likely needed more praying over than most, Prissie Seldom, who goes to all the funerals, and Increase, I don't suppose there were more than ten other people there when they finally put the box in the ground. I guess most of them just wanted to make sure she was dead and weren't that interested in getting her along to heaven afterward.

I've never really understood that bit, the part about praying for the dead to get them into heaven. Frankly, I'd have thought that was sort of like shutting the gate after the cows got loose, but Pastor Gather says it works. Which makes me wonder if perhaps Increase was more of my mind, that the dead don't know nothing, and that's why he did what he did when they were lowering her into the ground. I mean, if he didn't think it would do any harm, if he figured it was only a joke, then what Tilla did to him and his wife afterward wasn't really called for. The funeral was almost over when he did it, which leads me to think he sort of did it on impulse, not out of any real meanness or anything. Prissie had soaked two or three handkerchiefs before he did it, so you know it wasn't the first thing he did. Mr. Glover was watching him a bit, wondering what he was doing there in the first place, and he saw him rummaging about in his pockets for something, but he says Increase seemed to find that bit of salt almost by accident. As I've been known to carry my own lunch in my pockets, I can say for sure that it's easy enough to get a few grains of salt down there. Mr. Glover thinks Increase just happened to find it there, but once he had it in his hand he got a bit of badness in him and took advantage of the situation. Anyway, when it came time for us to drop a bit of dirt down in the grave, Increase tossed down that salt instead!

"There," he said, "that should keep you twisting for a while!"

Well, Prissie started wailing right off, even whacked Increase with a soggy handkerchief. Pastor wasn't too pleased with her or him. Increase got an earful from the preacher about bringing superstition into the proceedings, Prissie he sent on home because she was making such a racket. By the time that grave was filled in again, I'd say Prissie had told everyone in town about how poor Auntie Tilla wouldn't get any heavenly rest now, no matter how many people prayed for her, because Increase had salted her grave. Even the most God-fearing folk in town started looking at Increase a little funny then. I mean, everyone's heard that salting a grave will raise a ghost and, even if you didn't really believe it, well, it's just not a nice thing to do, is it?

Increase tried to laugh it off whenever anyone mentioned it to him, but you could see that the laughing wasn't always real. I think he was mad 'cause everyone took it so serious and he'd only meant it for a joke. I bet there were lots of times when he really regretted giving into the temptation, if not right away, then soon enough.

Mr. Glover was the one who first told me about the trouble. He and his missus were out to the Dwyer place for supper one evening—he and Increase were eyeing some plants that Increase had grown from seeds in the new catalog, and the women were just visiting—when they got the fright of their lives. Mrs. Glover had said that the house seemed tense even before supper. The Dwyers' maid was jumping at everything—or nothing, depending on how you looked at it—and Mrs. Dwyer insisted on having tea out on the porch even though it was sort of chilly that day. But she couldn't serve supper out there, so they all ended up inside eventually and that's when Mrs. Glover first heard it. A sharp wailing sound that got cut off in midwail was how Mrs. Glover described it to me. The

Dwyers tried to pretend like they hadn't heard anything, but that young girl they got working for them, she dropped the gravy boat right there on the dining room floor! Next, there was a knocking sound running all around the room, like someone was dragging a stick along the palings of a fence. But the worst, especially for Mrs. Glover, was the yelling. That's when she left, when the yelling got so you could hear a voice instead of just wailing.

"It was Auntie Tilla, sure as I'm standing here." When I asked her what the ghost was saying, she wasn't right sure. "Sounds kind of muffled at times, but I recognized her voice right away."

Now, I wouldn't say Mrs. Glover is a gossipy woman. She hears plenty behind the counter in the General, and don't speak a word of it to anyone, but this wasn't the usual sort of thing. I mean, it gave her a terrible fright. She was as pale as, well, pale as a ghost when she got back to town. I saw them go by on their way around back and I can tell you that neither of them looked too good. Mr. Glover was getting her a cup of tea when I came in to tell him I'd put the horses away. She was shaking like a leaf. If she'd been more recovered, she probably wouldn't have said anything. She's a discreet sort of woman, Mrs. Glover. But, she was scared and it all just tumbled out. According to her, and I've never known her to tell a lie, Mrs. Dwyer said all that knocking and wailing and yelling had been going on ever since Auntie Tilla got buried.

Word of something like that gets around town pretty quick.

Before long, people were going out to the Dwyer place just to see if they couldn't hear something for themselves. And as often as not, Tilla was more than willing to put on a show. After a while, once people satisfied themselves that it was really happening, you couldn't get anyone to go out there, especially after dark. Seems Tilla was more active after dark, she'd throw things at some people and let other people see her glowing in a corner or at the top of the stairs.

Pastor Gather claimed it was all a lot of superstitious foolishness, but he didn't spend any nights out there, either.

I can't recall anyone being surprised when Mrs. Dwyer died. Some people took it as something inevitable, a lot of people expressed regret, Mrs. Dwyer was a good woman, after all, and she hadn't done anything wrong, but no one seemed all that surprised when she fell down the stairs and broke her neck. That's when that young girl, the maid Dorcas, came to work at the General. She couldn't stay out at the Dwyer place anymore, and Mrs. Glover tends to take in strays. It was Dorcas that told us how bad things had gotten out there.

"Not a dish left unbroken, or a mirror left hanging. Whatever furniture that could be toppled was toppled and all Mr. Dwyer's beautiful books thrown off the shelves. Lamp wicks kept burning off. The food was all spoiling and the milk was souring even before I could bring it in from the barn! Was awful!" She shivered a lot then. "The worst was that voice, though. The things it'd say!"

This was the first anyone had heard about real words that anyone else could understand, so naturally everyone leaned forward a bit while they waited for her to go on. Even Mrs. Glover seemed to be anxious for that bit.

"Well, it were certainly Tilla." Dorcas began slowly. "I mean, she said things that we didn't understand at first, about 'being made small' and 'being parched.'"

I put in the bits about "shriveling" and she allowed as how that had been part of it too, so I knew for sure it was Tilla.

"Then she started demanding things."

Mrs. Glover blinked real hard at that. "Things? But what could a ghost want?"

Dorcas shrugged. "Well, I don't know, not really. Maybe 'things' isn't the right way to put it. She kept shouting about 'blessed sleep' and 'safety from ones such as me' and all sort of things like that."

Mr. Glover nodded then and sent the girl off to make more tea. To his wife he said, "Sounds like she's looking to rest in peace."

I don't normally say much to the Glovers. For starters, they don't ask me much. Then again, they always struck me as pretty sensible people who catch on to things without anyone having to point it out to them. I do ask them things, from time to time, and I wasn't getting the part about "safety from ones such as me." Was she saying that Increase had powwowed her after all, with that salt in the grave? I didn't think anyone could be a powwow without knowing he was one.

The Glovers never had much truck with powwowers, so they couldn't answer that for sure, but they admitted it sure sounded to them like

Increase had gotten himself into something he ought not to have. Whether he knew it when he was doing it, well, that they couldn't know at all.

Now, the Glovers never did say that Increase was a powwow man, but once the things Dorcas had been telling us started to get around, you could see people looking at him differently, making signs at him the way they used to at Tilla. He didn't take well to that, but what could he do?

It went on that way for months after Mrs. Dwyer died. Increase got so thin you could have used him for a toothpick and still had to root around some to get all the stuck bits out. I suppose, in the end, he didn't have much choice but to do what he did, get in that powwow man from out Pennsylvania, but that didn't make it look any better for him. The powwow man, though, he at least seemed to know what he was doing. He spent the night out at the Dwyers' place, talking things over with Aunt Tilla, and he told Increase everything that she told him.

Seems Auntie Tilla could probably have rested, even with that salt in her grave, if she hadn't been worrying about that tooth she lost when her face slammed into the steps. She wanted it back, buried with her in her own grave. Increase didn't see what a tooth had to do with anything, but that powwow man, he explained it all for him, how if some other powwower got hold of that, they could tie Auntie Tilla's ghost to them, use her magic for their hexes, keep her from resting in the afterlife. Until that tooth got buried with her, she was going to keep coming back at Increase, simple as that.

Well, whether he really believed in all that is still a question, but come the next morning, when I was out sweeping the porch, who did I find scrambling around on all fours but Increase. He was peering down through the boards, moving a lantern back and forth, looking for some sign of that tooth. I watched him for a long time. I think if he'd seen it down there, he'd have torn that porch to splinters, but of course he never did find it, not even after rooting around in the mud and droppings there in the street at the bottom of the steps. Would have been hard for him to find it down there when it was sitting in a mug in my own little room out behind the General.

I'd found it while I was sweeping up the day after Tilla died. I suppose I'd been thinking to bring it along to the undertaker before he finished boxing her up for the funeral, but with one thing and another, I'd sort of forgotten about it. When I saw Increase peering through the porch steps, I thought to maybe go out back and get it for him, but there was something about the way he was looking that morning, all frantic with his hair sticking up all over, that got me thinking twice. Sure, he might be glad enough to have it, eventually, but in the meantime I thought he might be angry enough at Tilla to feel the need to take some of that anger out on someone a little more substantial before he started feeling grateful. Still, I just might have gone and got it, maybe dropped it somewhere where Increase could find it, if I hadn't happened to hear what he was muttering under his breath! Yup, more of that "shriveling" stuff.

Now, I suppose any man under the pressure Increase was feeling might well say things he didn't rightly mean. I like to give any man the benefit of the doubt. Once or twice, I've even been known to take the Good Lord's name in vain myself, and mean nothing all that evil by it. So, it's possible that Increase was only making sounds without really meaning anything by it, but I wasn't completely sure. See, I couldn't help *thinking* while I was sweeping. Sweeping don't take much of a man's concentration really, does it? And, I couldn't help thinking about how Auntie Tilla just *happened* to slip in that patch of water after Increase waved his fingers at her. And wasn't it another real coincidence that Increase just *happened* to find salt in his pocket the day they buried Auntie Tilla? And, for that matter, seeing as I knew I had the tooth, why would Auntie Tilla be so all fired up to haunt Increase's place instead of my own little room?

I'd listened pretty close to everything the preacher and the Glovers and the Glovers' customers had been saying about Increase, but not a one of them seemed to think Increase was more than a nasty man who'd probably reaped what he'd sown in teasing Tilla so bad all these years. And maybe they were right. But like I said, I wasn't completely sure. Now, I don't know what I would have done if I hadn't seen that Pennsylvania powwower walking down the street after Increase took himself off home. Probably nothing. But, with him right there, I figured I might as well ask. So, on a bright sunny afternoon, me and the Pennsylvania powwower sat on the steps and talked a bit about Auntie Tilla and Increase Dwyer.

I didn't come right out and say as how I had the tooth out back. We chatted a bit about other things first. Like how I didn't see how prayers could make much difference to a person after they were dead. That Pennsylvania powwower pretty much agreed with me on that one. Turns out he pretty much agreed with me that Increase just "happened" to do an awful lot of odd things too. So, by the time I got around to mentioning that Auntie Tilla's tooth was in my room out back, that powwow man had come around to my way of thinking, that giving up that tooth might not be for the best at all.

"It could be that this Increase fellow is just what he seems," he said, and nodded to himself. "But then again, could be he's a whole lot more. I knew this powwow woman back in Pennsylvania. She was working all kinds of charms and hexes for years, right out in public most of the time—and no one the wiser until she died and they found all her stuff hidden around the house."

"You figure Increase could be one like that?"

"Well, it's hard to tell, isn't it?" I nodded. "Probably better off safe than sorry."

So we sat for a bit more, considering our problem.

"Can't just give him that tooth."

No, I agreed. If he was a powwow man, he'd be all the more trouble with all her power to draw on too.

"Can't just throw it under the bed."

No, I agreed. If he ever found out I had it, I'd be in trouble for sure.

"Can't just throw it away."

No, Auntie Tilla had her rights too, and it was, after all, her tooth.

Couldn't I just give it to him? Surely a powerful powwow man from Pennsylvania would know what to do with it.

"No, can't do that either. I'm a man, same as any other. Never know what temptations I've got to face yet. Could be, if I had it, that someday I'd want to use it myself."

You can always tell the really powerful powwow men, they have the knowing of things like that.

"No," he told me. "Best to just hexen the darn thing and give it back to Tilla."

Now, I had no intention of digging up the grave of a powwow woman, even if she did want her tooth back, and I told him that right away, but as it turns out that wasn't what he had in mind at all.

It was nearly midnight when we two strolled out to the Dwyer place. I didn't hear any wailing and banging myself, but then again I never went inside either. The powwow man from Pennsylvania, he stuck his head inside for a few minutes, just to make sure that Auntie Tilla knew it was us wandering around, so she wouldn't get up to no bad high jinks, and to see for himself that Increase was at home. He was, so we two got down to business right away.

That powwow man, who was called Rheinhold Rehmeyer in public— I never asked his powwow name—had spent most of the afternoon working on the hex for that tooth. What he showed me didn't look like much, a bundle of twigs tied together with some old bits of cloth, which he said came from one of Increase's old shirts that his missus had rel-

egated to wash-bucket rags. It looked mostly like a bird nest that someone had picked apart and then tied together in a neat little package. I
didn't ask what he'd said over the bundle, of course, that wasn't any of
my concern, and he probably wouldn't have told me if I did ask. I just
watched as he undid it a bit and held it out for me to stick the tooth
down inside. When he took out a great big woodsman's knife and told
me to hold out my hand, though, I made sure to ask him what he was
about before doing any such thing.

"It needs some blood from Tilla to seal the hexing." When I pointed
out that might be a mite difficult, what with Tilla being dead and all, he
just looked at me like I was soft in the head. "I know that, boy, but what
flowed in her veins flows in yours too, right?"

I must have looked a bit startled then. Most folk 'round that way had
more or less forgotten that me and Tilla was related. Other people called
her Auntie because she was known to be a powwow woman, but I called her
Auntie because she was one—mine. Not that we were real close or anything.
Powwow people mostly keep to themselves and I'd been with the Glovers
since my own ma died. I don't know how that man from Pennsylvania knew
it, but like I said the real powerful ones did tend to know things. He was
waiting with the knife, looking more impatient by the second, so rather
than ask how he came to know that, I just kept my mouth shut and held
out my hand.

It didn't hurt much. A quick little jab in that skin between the thumb
and the rest of the fingers was all it was. It didn't even bleed much. He

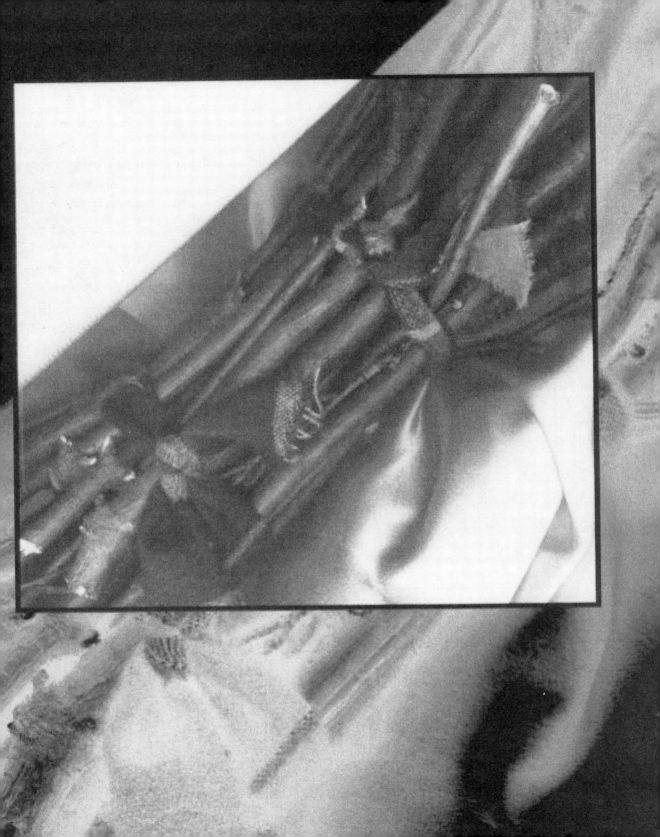

milked my hand a bit to make sure the tooth was well coated before he let me go. After tying the bundle back together again, he jerked his head toward the house. "Now, you just go and bury that there in front of the door."

"Me?"

"Well of course you. Wouldn't be any good for me to do it, would it? Then I'd know where it was and I could come back and dig it up anytime I wanted."

I hadn't thought about that, hadn't thought I'd be the one out there in the moonlight digging up Increase's front yard! I had to readjust my thinking a little at that point, so to settle my nerves a bit I turned the bundle over a few times like I was looking it over for spaces the tooth might fall out through. There weren't any, it was made sturdy, but it gave me a few minutes to think. "I thought we were going to give it back to Tilla?"

"Well, you don't really think she's back in that hole in the ground, do you? With her out here shouting her head off every night?" He chuckled. "We gonna bury that tooth right out here where she is. Up to her what she does with it then."

That chuckle gave me goose bumps. "What do you mean 'does with it'?"

He patted my arm and shoved me toward the wide open yard. "Go on now, quick, before midnight passes. I'm gonna stroll on down the road, so you'll know I don't see where you put it. I'll meet you back behind the General."

Left: Bundles, or "boodles" as they're known in some eastern states, were buried near doorways in North America as well as Europe and Asia. A clay jar or wicker basket might be substituted for the stick bundle, and the contents could range from a lock of hair from the first child born in the house to the skeleton of the first cat to die in the house. Whatever the contents, finding an exposed bundle was the worst sort of luck. A death in the house—or tent—would certainly fit those expectations.

I wasn't sure exactly what I was looking for in a good spot to bury the bundle, somewhere in front of the door was all I'd been told, so I spent a bit of time walking back and forth out there before deciding to sit on the bottom step of the porch and do my digging from there. I looked up from time to time, but I didn't see anyone watching. About six inches down, I ran into a flat stone and I realized I'd hit the base rock Increase must have set down to support the posts for the steps. Moving out a few inches, I found the edge, dug under it a bit, and shoved the bundle in there. No way anyone would dig that up by accident.

I was just patting the last of the dirt from my hands—I'd already dragged my shoe over the spot a few times so no one would notice it being different than anywhere else in the yard—when I heard Tilla. An awful sound it was, like someone was skinning a live cat and laughing the whole while. I was beating it across the yard for the bushes when the door flew open behind me. One look at Increase's wild face was enough for me to pick up my heels a little faster. I should have been looking where I was going, but somehow the idea of turning my back on Increase didn't appeal. I was looking right at him when he hit the porch running, saw him come flying down the steps full speed. He didn't trip, didn't fall, didn't step on his boot lace or anything like that. He just slammed into empty air! Went to leap off that bottom step and was brought up solid against nothing at all. He couldn't have hit any harder if he'd run into a wall. Knocked himself completely backward, measured his whole length back onto the steps. I think he must have knocked himself senseless there for a few minutes. I'd made it to the bushes alongside the road before he found his footing again. Not that it made much difference to him. Try as he might, he couldn't get off that step.

The harder he tried, the louder Tilla laughed. I stood there, staring, until I heard the sound of that Pennsylvania powwow man coming back along the road again. Then the two of us watched together for a time. Increase finally gave up. He sat on that step and sobbed his heart out while Tilla's laughing got louder and louder.

"He knows," the powwow man said as he leaned back against a tree. "Tilla decided to use that tooth of hers and now he can't leave there ever again. He'll likely starve eventually."

I leaned back too, not sure I understood what he was saying, not sure he'd answer if I asked. "She did that?"

"Yup. She didn't have to, you know. But it was her tooth, up to her what she did with it." He rubbed his chin thoughtfully. "I figured that's what would happen, why she wanted the tooth back so bad. Would have been sort of poetic justice if she'd convinced Increase himself to bring it back, wouldn't it?"

"What if someone dug it up again?"

He stared at me, real hard. "I wouldn't advise that, boy, I surely wouldn't. It was Tilla's choice. She didn't just tie him there, you know. He'll escape, eventually, no man lives forever, but she tied herself there, too."

"Until he dies."

"Don't matter if he dies or not, or when. Tilla's dead, she had to tie some bit of her spirit self to that bit of tooth in order to keep him inside. She can't never leave there!"

I wasn't sure which seemed worse, that Tilla would let that fellow starve to death inside his own house or that she'd been willing to tie herself to that place just to make his life even more miserable. In any case, no one ever did see Increase alive after that. I think the folk in Bedlam figured he *was* a powwower, and everyone knows how odd them pow-wow men are, so no one would have thought to go out to the Dwyer place right away.

When a week passed and no one had seen him, though, I started thinking about him, perhaps starving out there, and, after the Glovers closed the General one night, I took a pail of food out that way. I figured to leave it on the step, close enough that Increase could get it. I was right on that bottom step when I saw that the door was flapping in the wind. First I'd thought it was Tilla and I'd been ready to run, then I saw the way that door was moving with the breeze instead of against it. I hadn't heard anything up until now, so I guess I was a little braver than I might have been if she was still wailing away out there. I crept up those steps and stood close enough to catch the door when it blew open again. Seeing Increase just inside damn near stopped my heart right there, but between one beat and the next, I realized he wouldn't be doing me any harm.

Like the door, he was sort of swaying in the breeze. Must have took him a while to die. He hadn't measured the rope out quite right and his toes were just skimming the ground. Despite that, he'd managed to kill himself right enough, looked even worse than Tilla had after she broke her face all over the General's steps.

Now, I'm not known for any particular wisdom, but it didn't take no powwow man to figure that going back to town and trying to explain how Increase came to have hung himself in his own house wasn't going to do anything good for me, so I just took my pail and myself back to my own little room behind the General and did my best to look surprised when someone else came into the store with the news nearly a month later.

After that, I sort of put the whole thing out of my mind. No one ever heard much from Tilla after that either. A few families tried living in the old Dwyer place, but no one ever stayed for long. I used to think I'd go back and dig up that old tooth some day, see it settled in Tilla's grave with her, but time passed on without anyone, including me, taking any special note of it. Me and Dorcas got married a few summers after Auntie Tilla died and I was so busy raising a family that I never realized that those new houses outside town were built right over the Dwyer holding. I don't know if I could even find that old tooth now, without the old house to use as a marker. I don't suppose I'd be remembering it at all if I hadn't got this letter asking for permission to move Auntie Tilla's remains. Seems the town is growing too fast for itself to keep up with. They need that cemetery land for some new road. They want to know if I'd mind them moving Auntie Tilla to a new graveyard the other side of town.

"'Course I don't," I told Dorcas. "It's not like Auntie Tilla was ever really in there anyway, is it?"

Not with that tooth out there somewhere.

The custom of burying bundles of bones, or teeth, or even the whole skeleton of some small animal under the doorway of a new house was once common in the eastern American states and, to a lesser degree, in the eastern provinces of Canada. Almost any builder in any eastern town can remember finding such a bundle themselves or hearing of some other work crew that stumbled over one. It has become the normal practice to simply re-inter the bundles as close to the old location as possible. If asked what the bundles were originally designed to do, the usual answer is either "to keep good luck inside the house" or, alternatively, "to keep whatever's ill outside." The custom is frequently cited as being Dutch in origin, which may explain its long folkloric association with communities in Pennsylvania and, by further extrapolation, with the so-called powwow belt, an area famous for its population of "witches."

At this remove in time, it's impossible to know how much of "The Bedlam Witch" tale is true and how much is the invention of storytellers who took a local legend and built up the first person–styled story that has become a Halloween staple throughout the mountain areas in the

East. However, a Rheinhold Rehmeyer did live in the Carolinas in 1723; he was arrested there for cutting purses, and, just over two hundred years later, in 1928, his great-great-grandson, Nelson Rehmeyer, was killed while trying to protect a spell book. His murderers' trials are matters of public record.

"The Witch Danced" is another story of a witch reaching back from beyond the grave to wreak physical as well as psychological terror. This one hails from Maine, where it was recounted at "UnCONventional Wisdom," a folklore festival, in 1988. The storyteller, Aaron Delacroix, related similar occult fables heard in his home state of Louisiana as well as a gender-reversed version he encountered in Vermont. He chose "The Witch Danced" as his entry in the Maine symposium because once when he was a child his family vacationed in Maine, and it was in that state that someone had actually pointed out the headstone with its unexplainable markings.

The Witch Danced

Esme Black was beautiful, the most beautiful woman anyone could ever remember seeing in Brookside, Maine. She spoke French and Italian, painted the most delicate portraits, played at least a dozen musical instruments, and could sing fit to shame the birds. Yet, it wasn't for any of those accomplishments that Esme was truly known. Esme Black was also the most wonderful dancer Brookside had ever seen. She floated at the end of a man's arm, her feet barely touching the floor, her steps pure grace. Any man lucky enough to partner her for even a single dance thought he'd gone to heaven for as long as the music played. So, when Esme began dancing more and more often with Gerald Brousseau, he was generally considered to be a lucky young man, and many male hearts were broken when, just before Christmas, Esme and Gerald announced their upcoming marriage.

At first, the couple seemed touched by a special blessing. Gerald's business, a small shipyard, received an order that would keep two shifts of workers busy for nearly two years and make Gerald a tidy income in the process. Esme's uncle sent the girl a trousseau from Paris that would be the envy of any bride. Investments made by Esme's father turned an unexpected profit and, to celebrate, he bought a brand-new home for the happy pair. If a fairy godmother had landed on the couple's wedding cake and offered to grant them their fondest wish, neither of them would have known what more they could possibly ask for.

Nor were they stingy with their happiness, drawing a wide circle of friends and relatives into a round of parties and dances. Human nature being what it is, you might well have expected there to be some rot amid so much happiness, someone somewhere who coveted their wealth or their happiness—but there wasn't! Adored by everyone they met, Esme and Gerald spent as many hours in charitable works as they did in their own pursuit of enjoyment. When Esme received a letter from Belle, her only cousin, saying she would indeed be thrilled to come from France to help Esme prepare for the wedding, Esme was ecstatic and Gerald smiled often at seeing her so happy.

Belle's arrival was all that Esme had hoped. Her cousin, almost her twin in appearance, was Esme's only female relative and Esme delighted is sharing all those small, feminine confidences with her while choosing fabric for this and flowers for that. Belle, for her part, smiled frequently and, after proving herself nearly as good a dancer as her cousin, proceeded to bring smiles back to the faces of many of those disappointed young men.

Only one person failed to take to Belle immediately. Gerald, though he never spoke ill of her or criticized any of her actions, nevertheless often frowned when he found himself seated next to her or was forced by the niceties of polite society to partner her during a dance. What it was about her that bothered him, he couldn't seem to clarify, not to himself and not to Esme, who couldn't help but notice the growing coolness between her fiancé and her cousin.

The first harsh words ever spoken between Gerald and Esme were over Belle when, without any explanation, Gerald left Belle alone on the dance floor. Belle's embarrassment was plain to see in the high color that flooded her face before she could escape to a dimly lit corner of the room. When Esme found her and asked what had happened, Belle could only shake her head. "We were just dancing. I reached up to brush a loose hair from his collar and he acted as if I'd slapped his face! He—he just walked off."

When Gerald refused to explain, Esme, bewildered and dismayed, turned to her father for advice. It was some days later before Jack Black could engineer a private meeting with his soon-to-be son-in-law, but knowing how upset the situation was making his daughter, he waited up quite late one evening until Gerald returned from the busy boatyard. At first Gerald denied that there was anything wrong, a position he would have maintained had the questioner been one bit less stubborn. Under Jack's pointed questions, however, Gerald finally admitted that his problem wasn't that he disliked Belle at all—in fact, he liked her all too well!

As Jack listened, a sobbing, clearly heartbroken Gerald confessed that, ever since Belle's arrival, he'd been tormented by erotic dreams of his fiancée's cousin, that whenever he danced with Belle he completely forgot the beautiful woman who was to become his wife. It wasn't that he wanted to lose himself in the French girl's charms, he simply couldn't help it! If Gerald were snubbing Belle, it was only his last-ditch effort to save his relationship with Esme.

When Gerald had finally finished his confession, Jack poured them both a stiff drink and urged the younger man to a seat before the fire while he gave some thought to the rather bizarre predicament with which he was now faced. "You say you've never looked at another woman until now?"

"Never! I love Esme, truly I do."

Jack nodded once, then continued his thinking and drinking. Eventually, he sighed and, staring deeply into his glass, began to tell a story of his own. "Many years ago, when I was wooing Esme's mother, I chanced to overhear her talking with her sister, Belle's mother. Belle's mother evidently thought my relationship with her sister was proceeding too slowly and she was anxious for Esme's mother to try a charm her own mother claimed was most useful in capturing a recalcitrant young man's attention. Esme's mother, of course, was well aware of my feelings for her and laughed off her sister's offer."

Gerald's hands tightened around his glass. "And you think Belle is using her mother's charm on me?"

"I fear it, yes."

The relief on Gerald's face was evident. "Thank God! All this time, I've been castigating myself for a spineless cad when it's been some witchery I had no part in at all!"

"Unfortunately, I doubt that mere knowledge can save you."

Gerald's shoulders slumped again. "Then I'm damned already?" His eyes closed. "Then I must leave here immediately. I am determined that no act of mine shall bring sadness or disgrace to Esme."

Jack topped off the younger man's glass once more. "Perhaps it is not as dark as all that yet. If Esme's mother was still with us, we could ask her what might prove useful against this charm but, as she's not, we'll have to make do with what small amount of information I still recall and see if we can't break this charm."

"Then you know what it is? How it works?"

"Not in great detail, but I remember it was described as a knot of hair woven in a particular fashion."

"Which explains why Belle was always so anxious to remove any stray hair from my clothes!" Gerald jumped up in his excitement. "Then all we need do is find the charm and destroy it!"

That proved more difficult to do than say, and despite their best efforts, neither man was able to find the charm they knew must be hidden where Belle would have easy access to it. When they met again several nights later, it had become obvious that further steps must be taken to retrieve it. "We shall have to confront Belle herself, reveal what we know, and demand that she return the charm to us," Jack decided.

"She'll refuse."

"Then we shall have no choice but to turn her over to the law."

Gerald sank into the deep chair by the fireside and let his head fall into his hands. "They'll hang her for witchcraft."

"Perhaps, but you and Esme will have each other."

As Gerald had predicted, Belle refused to produce the charm that had so addled the young man's senses, refused to even admit that such a charm existed. Her pretty face turned ugly as she suggested that it was no spell of hers that caused his eyes to waver. "You allow yourself to lust after another woman, then blame *her* for your sin!"

The magistrate, however, didn't see it that way, pointing to Gerald's spotless reputation as proof that only some outside agent could possibly have interfered with what was so obviously a case of true love. The jury found against Belle in just ten minutes. The judge took less than five to sentence her to hanging on the public gallows within the week.

The next day, Esme, distraught at the horrible end awaiting her cousin, went to the jail to plead with her to confess her sin, turn over the charm, and beg for extradition back to France. "I'm sure my father can influence the judge, if you'll only confess and repent!"

Belle, however, only spat in Esme's face, calling her a fool for tying herself to a man so easily led astray.

At that, even Esme's much-touted sympathy failed her. "I would have preferred that you dance at my wedding rather than at the end of a rope, Belle, but if that is your choice, I will do nothing to prevent it."

"I may dance at the end of a rope, sweet cousin, but not before I dance on your grave!"

Esme's face paled and she swayed on her feet. Her father, who had allowed her to come only to convince her of her cousin's betrayal, swore loudly and pulled Esme from the jail.

That evening, Esme retreated to her bed early, claiming a headache from the pressure of the last few days. Gerald and her father wished her a speedy recovery, neither of them giving any credence to Belle's last words. Esme was a perfectly healthy young woman, and there was absolutely no reason to expect her to do anything other than wake up the next morning rested and recovered from her unpleasant interview.

Which was precisely why her death, discovered the following morning, was such a shock.

Belle's imminent execution was almost forgotten as family and friends gathered to comfort one another and, in a few days, see Esme's body laid to rest. The marker covering the grave was the palest pink granite, beautiful and strong, just as Esme had been. The day after Esme's funeral, Belle was hanged but Gerald wasn't there to see it. Instead, while Jack went to ensure that no last-minute reprieve would save the woman he believed responsible for his daughter's death, Gerald went to lay fresh flowers on Esme's grave, a task he'd sworn to continue daily for the rest of his life.

Though it was impossible to be sure, the two men would later come to agree that the rusty footprint that rose on the face of the stone as Gerald changed the flowers appeared just minutes before Belle's feet left the floor of the gallows platform and began their very last dance.

No amount of rubbing or scrubbing could remove that mark from Esme's gravestone. As soon as it was washed away, the rust-colored water, which some said looked like old blood, would seep its way up through the solid rock and remain there, a sharp, distinct impression of a woman's tiny foot. Even removing the stone and replacing it with a new one proved useless. Each and every stone, within moments of being laid, would begin to discolor.

Eventually, father and fiancé admitted their impotence.

The stone was removed altogether.

Left: Numerous gravestones are said to bear some imprint of the deceased. One Texas marker supposedly bleeds on the anniversary of its owner's death. This eastern example, over "Kickin' Kate," traces the dancer's high-kicking leg.

in burkittsville

Creating a sense of place was evidently high on the list of priorities when the cast and crew of *The Blair Witch Project* descended on Burkittsville, Maryland. Even though their story was a complete fiction, and the township of Blair never existed, they grounded their tale in a real community with real people, real grave markers, and, of course, a real location and a real name: Burkittsville. A very old adage says that the best place to hide a lie is between two truths; Dan Myrick and Ed Sánchez hid the fic-

tional town of Blair beneath the real town of Burkittsville—a decision that hasn't met with universal gratitude there.

One reason is, not unexpectedly, the vandalism and harassment the film brought to a small community that had been given no warning (one reason why location-filming permits are required) they were about to be thrust into the limelight.

A second reason, however, was that while Sánchez, Myrick, and company co-opted those portions of Burkittsville that they wanted to use and fictionalized much more, they ignored the history and legend that made Burkittsville, the *real* Burkittsville, special to its residents. There may never have been a Blair Witch in the hills around Burkittsville, but the town's history is pretty interesting in its own right.

This last legend, then, while not a witch tale, is an intrinsic part of the

Above: Visitors to Burkittsville won't be having their pictures taken next to the town's original sign anymore. That one, an antique, was stolen. Fortunately, vandalism at the Union Cemetery, where other footage for *The Blair Witch Project* was shot, has been less acquisitive.

place that helped inspire *The Blair Witch Project.* Surprisingly, there are echoes of the Blair Witch tale, proving once again how powerful is the connection between the images chosen for *The Blair Witch Project* and the images that have haunted American occult folklore for nearly three hundred years. Some things just don't change. . . .

The Confederate Soldiers and Spook Hill

As is only to be expected in an area where layer after layer of history was laid down on the surrounding ground, Burkittsville has a lively array of events from which to draw its local legends and, occasionally, characters from several different eras will happily commingle to produce an even more colorful tale. The story of "The Confederate Soldiers at Spook Hill" is just such a commingling.

Though almost every stretch of territory claims some connection to the Civil War, Burkittsville's association with one particular event, the Battle for Crampton's Gap, is noteworthy for the way circumstances overtook the community. Keeping in mind that modern-day Burkittsville boasts a population of only a few souls over two hundred, picture the scene when this tiny town was inundated by *seventeen thousand* Confederate soldiers. Homes became forward command posts, then barracks, and, when the battles turned from moment to moment, field hospitals for soldiers of both sides. Miraculously, few of those buildings, dating back to 1862, were harmed.

In a real sense, the Burkittsville of today is little changed from the Burkittsville of the Civil War era. Real people still live in those homes and, in many cases, can tell you who slept, died, or just passed the odd day of peace in which room of their house. When history happens literally under your roof, it takes on an immediacy impossible to replicate in any textbook. Which probably explains why a local optical illusion has long been attributed to the ghosts of the soldiers who lived and died in Burkittsville.

In September of 1862, Confederate and Union soldiers were inching closer to an inevitable meeting at Crampton's Gap. From the south, Confederate soldiers were hauling in heavy arms including wagon-mounted cannons that were pulled into position by men as well as animals. From the north, Union men trekked southward. There was nowhere to turn aside, no way to avoid the confrontation. On the evening before the encounter, commanders on both sides were planning swift actions to commence at dawn. While the cannons could inflict mass damage, they were clumsy, heavy, and tough to haul uphill. The Union soldiers, carrying light arms, mostly rifles, moved fast and easy over their side of the mountain. The Confederate losses were monstrous. Yet, amid the smoke, the stench, and the blood, the Confederate soldiers continued their apparently hopeless efforts to haul those cannons up into clear terrain. Most died in the process.

Years later, when a stretch of road leading out of Burkittsville began tricking the eyes of the town's residents, an occult rather than scientific explanation started circulating.

Like Magnetic Hill in New Brunswick or Gravity Hill in Pennsylvania, Spook Hill, as the road has come to be known, has a combination of characteristics that can fool human perceptions into believing that a car, stopped in the middle of the hill, will actually roll *up it*. Science, and the experience of thousands of drivers at less "haunted" sites, tell us that there's a rational explanation for the trick. In general, the inner ear, which regulates balance, also tells us if we're going up or going down, but that's not our only clue. Everyone has had the experience of sitting in a parked car and, out of the corner of their eye, seeing another vehicle pull ahead. Just for a second, until the logical half of our brain kicks in, we feel like we're sliding or falling backward.

Other tricks of the eye that can fool the ear? A hidden, or tilted, horizon. An object or row of objects that don't fit our visual preconceptions. For example, a row of trees marching off into the distance should, if they are all the same size, give the impression that those trees farthest away are smaller than those close at hand. If the trees aren't the same size, however, our perceptions change and we may not be able to judge our relative position as well. If those trees have grown into a leaning position due to the predominance of one prevailing wind direction, our sense of where the horizon should be is, once again, skewed. Any or all of these conditions can convince even the most skeptical observer that something is out of whack.

On Spook Hill, however, a more romantic explanation catches the imagination of residents and tourists alike: the feeling that you're moving uphill is not an illusion at all but brought about by the ghosts of hundreds of Confederate soldiers still trying to push those gun-wagons up that hill.

And, if not for the experience of Florence Dettwiller of Frederick County, most people would be happy enough to take the more romantic explanation as nothing more than that, a bit of local color.

Florence Dettwiller was no more gullible than any other thirty-six-year-old physics teacher checking out a possible field-trip location. Spook Hill, less than forty miles from the high school where she taught, was a natural fit with her unit on optical illusion. So, on a sunny morning in August, just before school was due to open, she and a friend, Tyler Jenkins, set out for a day trip that would take them through Burkittsville.

The drive was pleasant but, as often happens in the driest month of the year, dusty. Luckily, Ms. Dettwiller wasn't the only one preparing for the new school year and, just outside Burkittsville, they found a school team raising travel money with a hand car wash. Two dollars and ten minutes later, with directions from the kids on how to get to Spook Hill, Florence and Tyler drove through Burkittsville. The setup was much like the one Florence had seen at Magnetic Hill in New Brunswick, though

Right: Ghostly handprints are said to haunt any number of sites where violent deaths occurred. The Tower of London, the Bastille, and Devil's Island all claim prints that can only be seen under special circumstances.

much less commercial. She ran through it the first time with Tyler in the car with her. Both admitted the illusion was solid, even when they'd figured out which elements of their surroundings were contributing to it. Just to see how it looked from the outside, Florence had brought along a video camera. After she'd repositioned the car at the beginning of the run, she gave Tyler the camera and had him tape her second pass. Which is when everything got decidedly unromantic.

There were no ghostly images on Florence Dettwiller's tape, no spooky sounds or sparkling light. The tape was perfectly normal. No, it was something as simple as dirt that made a teacher of physics a romantic.

The car had been washed less than an hour ago. Both Florence and Tyler had seen it cleaned. Being too hot to sit in an unmoving vehicle, they'd stood outside during the actual washing and would have sworn that every inch of the car had been scrubbed. The video camera that Tyler used had been in the trunk the entire drive, so when Florence retrieved it between her first and second run through Spook Hill, she'd had to open the trunk. Her car was a cheery yellow, the best possible color for showing dirt.

When she removed the camera, the trunk had been as clean as the rest of the car.

When she went to return it, dozens of handprints covered the trunk and bumper.

Not the tiny handprints of children, but the prints of men.

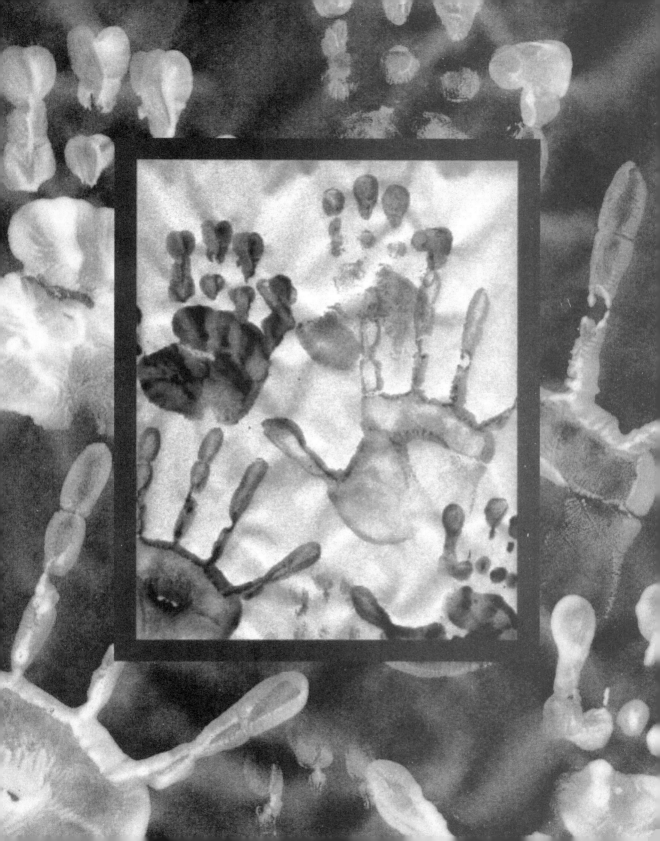

about the author

N.E. Genge is the author of numerous books, incuding *The Buffy Chronicles, Urban Legends,* and *The Unofficial X-Files Companion.* She lives in Labrador City, Newfoundland.